Contents

Any words appearing in the text in bold, **like this**, are explained in the Glossary.

Making colours

Our eyes can see thousands of colours, some bright, some of them dark. Red, yellow and blue are called **primary colours**. They cannot be made by mixing together other colours.

How many different colours do you think there are?

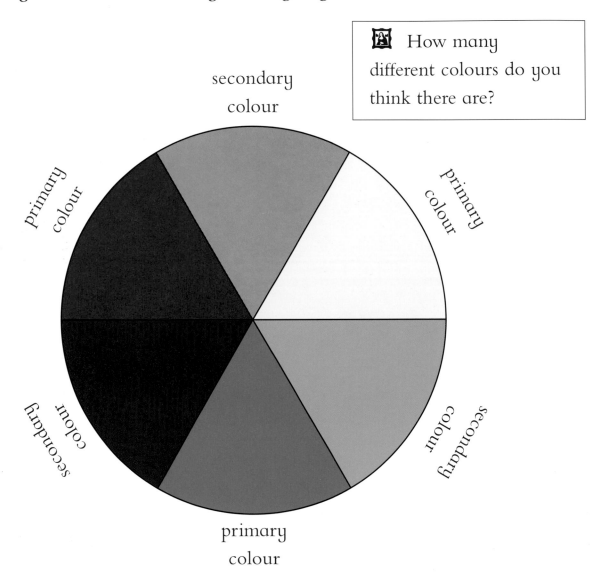

secondary colour

primary colour

primary colour

secondary colour

secondary colour

primary colour

Primary colours can be mixed to make every other colour.

Secondary colours are made by mixing two primary colours together. By adding more of one colour you get different **shades**. If you mix all three primary colours together you get a muddy brown!

You mix two primary colours together to make secondary colours.

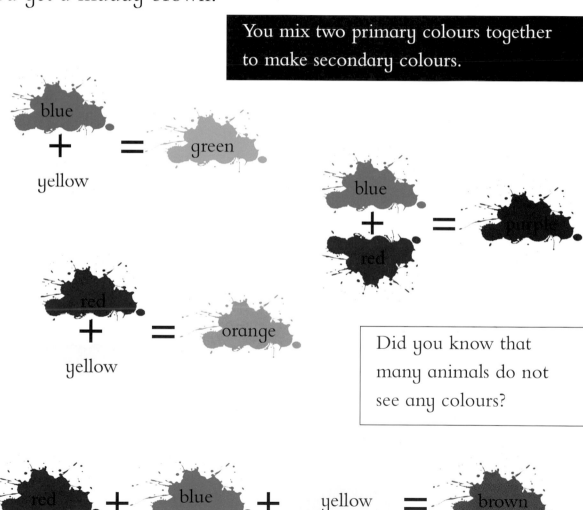

Did you know that many animals do not see any colours?

Colour partners

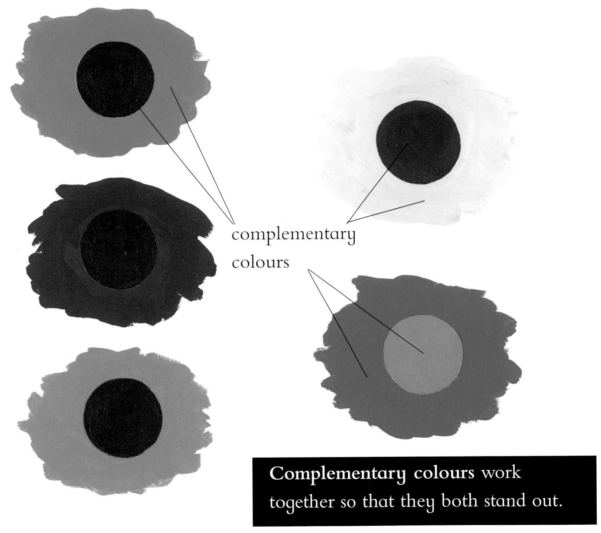

complementary colours

Complementary colours work together so that they both stand out.

Look at the colour wheel on page 4 again. Opposite colours **complement** one another. This means that they both stand out. Look at the red blobs on this page. All three are exactly the same but the one on the green background seems much brighter than the others.

6

Vincent van Gogh was a Dutch painter who lived from 1853 to 1890.

green background

dark hat

wavy beard

dark coat

Vincent van Gogh, *Portrait of the Postman Joseph Roulin*, 1889.

Van Gogh is well known for his use of complementary colours. The face of the postman stands out because the green background **contrasts** with the dark hat and coat and the wavy beard.

Warm and cool colours

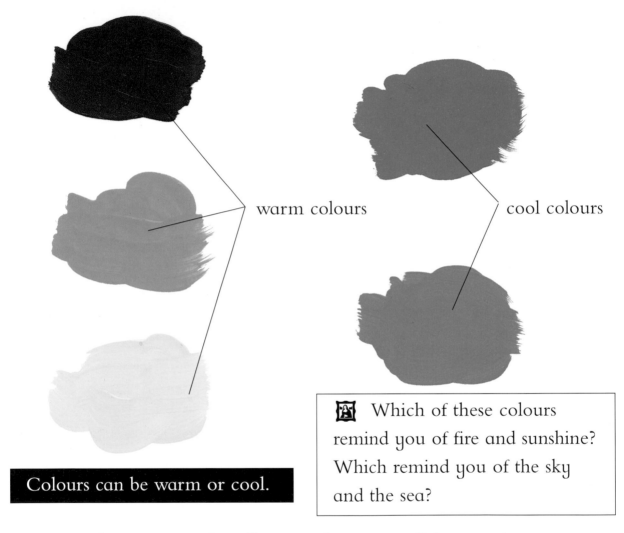

warm colours

cool colours

Colours can be warm or cool.

Which of these colours remind you of fire and sunshine? Which remind you of the sky and the sea?

Warm colours are red, yellow and orange. Often artists use these colours to show strong feelings. Cool colours are blue and green. When artists use cool colours their pictures can seem cold and lacking in feeling.

The French artist Paul Cézanne used warm colours to give his pictures great strength. Here he has put fruit on a white cloth with **earth colours** around it. The warm colours make the ordinary objects seem extra special.

Warm colours bring a **scene** to life.

cloth   apples   jug

Paul Cézanne, *Apples and Oranges*, 1895–1900.

Colour makes a difference!

hieroglyphs

This picture shows Egyptian hieroglyphic letters.

Can you make your writing more interesting by using different colours?

Look at these ancient Egyptian letters, which we call **hieroglyphs**. The walls of the tombs of kings were often covered with writing like this. The yellows, greens and browns make the writing more **decorative**.

Rose Window, Notre Dame Cathedral, Paris, France, about 1250.

Look at the date of this window. How old is it?

Stained glass has been used in churches for hundreds of years. Light is flooding through the glass in this window and filling the inside of the church with bright colours. People standing beneath the window can be covered with rainbow colours.

How artists use colour

Artists use colour in many ways. This painting is by an artist called Mark Rothko. He used big blocks of colour with fuzzy edges to show different moods and feelings. This kind of art is called **abstract**. It uses only colour and shape to make the picture.

Mark Rothko, *White Cloud Over Purple*, 1957.

How does this painting make you feel?

Henri Matisse made this picture when he was over 80 years old. His helpers painted large sheets of paper, and Matisse cut them into shapes and then stuck them onto **canvas**. He wanted to **explore** the difference between drawing objects, and making them with colour.

Why do you think Matisse called this picture *The Snail*?

Henri Matisse, *The Snail*, 1953.

13

Colour adds meaning

angel
Gabriel

Mary

Fra Angelico, *The Annunciation*, 1437–45.

In this painting, the angel Gabriel is telling Mary that she will give birth to Jesus, the Son of God. Look closely at Gabriel's wings. The blue and orange feathers **complement** one another, and so do the red clothes and green grass. Here colour is being used to help express deep religious feelings.

In Australia, around 200 years ago, the **Aboriginals** had their land taken from them by people from Europe. In the 1980s a group of 43 artists made this forest of hollow log bone-coffins. It shows ancient **designs** in natural **earth colours** to celebrate the Aboriginal culture.

Some of these hollow log bone-coffins are more than 3 metres tall. Measure 3 metres to see how big they are.

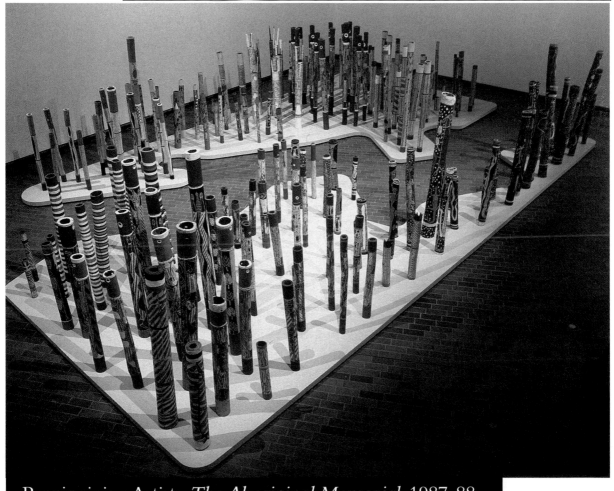

Ramingining Artists, *The Aboriginal Memorial*, 1987-88.

Colours in balance

The French artist Claude Monet was interested in the effect of light. He painted many pictures of the same places at different times of the day. In this beautiful painting he has balanced the blue light of early evening in winter, with an orange sky. This creates a feeling of great peace.

Claude Monet, *Haystacks: Snow Effect*, 1891.

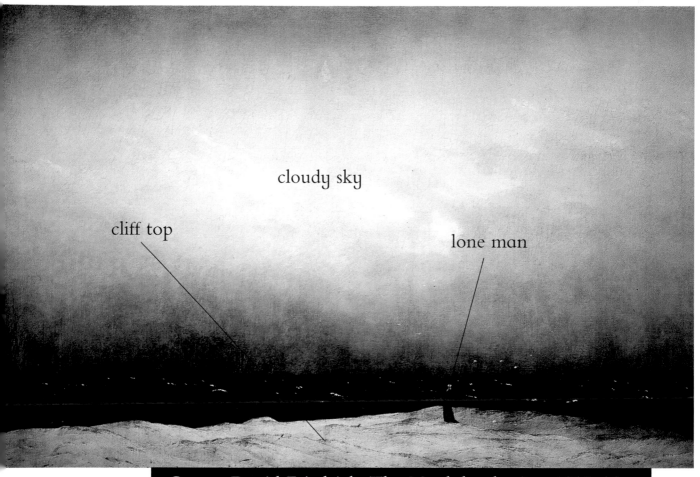

cloudy sky

cliff top

lone man

Caspar David Friedrich, *The Monk by the Sea*, 1808–10.

In this painting we can see a cloudy sky reflected on the a bare cliff top. The blue **tones** weave together to give a feeling of space. The lone man seems so small, set against the huge sky.

Colours that shout!

Joan Miró, *Figures in the Night*, 1960.

Think about the title of this painting. Would you want to be alone on a night like this?

Colours can be used in ways which surprise us. In this picture, dark night-time shapes are surrounded by strong splashes of colour which seem to leap off the **canvas**. But these bright **tones** are held in check by a mysterious darkness.

18

Edvard Munch, *The Scream*, 1893.

Bold colours are used again here, to make the painting strong.
Swirling **shades** of red and orange push out from the **canvas**.
The bright colours add to the excitement of the painting.

Colour and the modern world

This was one of Piet Mondrian's last paintings. All his life he **experimented** with the **primary colours**. He painted **abstract** pictures using yellow, red and blue. He also used grey and white blocks, and black lines to separate them.

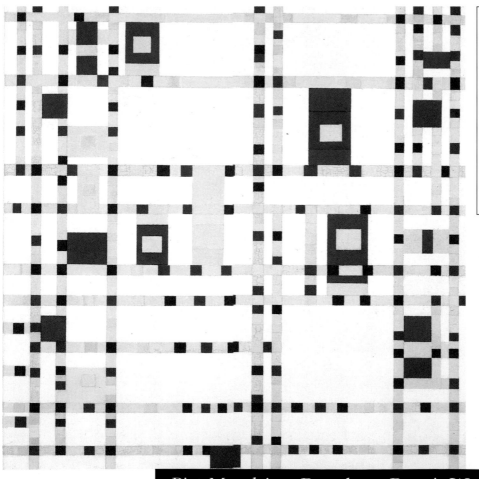

The straight lines of New York City's streets gave Mondrian the idea for this painting.

Piet Mondrian, *Broadway Boogie Woogie*, 1942–43.

Did you know that you can use the computer to send pictures you have made to a friend in another country? Have you ever done this?

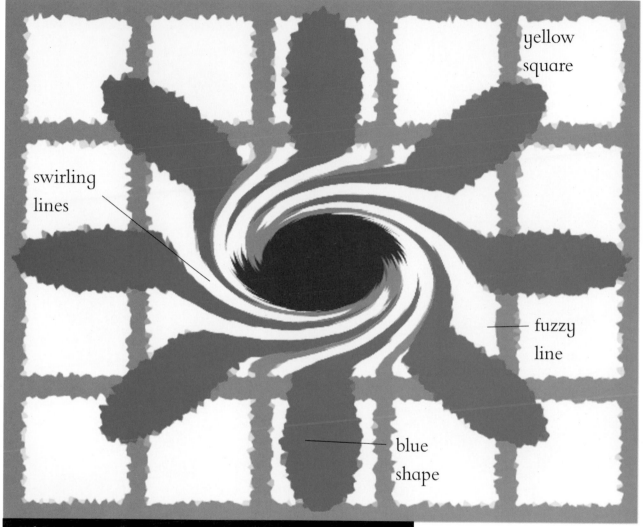

yellow square

swirling lines

fuzzy line

blue shape

This picture has been made using a computer.

Today we can use computers to make pictures. Colours, lines and shapes can be changed quickly and you can repeat patterns easily. If you have a good printer the results can be very exciting.

Mixing colours

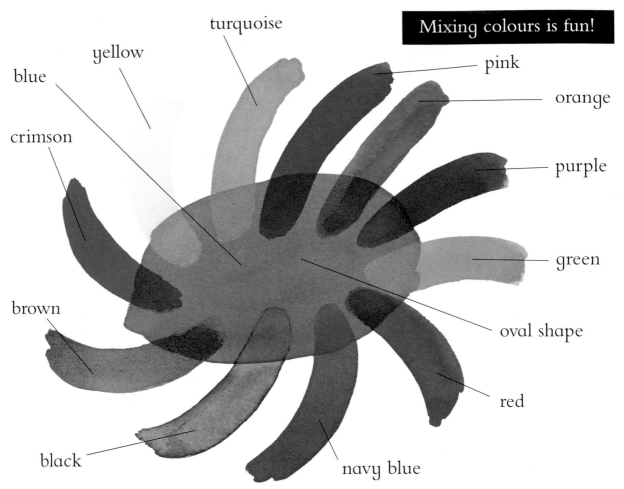

turquoise

yellow

blue

crimson

pink

orange

purple

green

brown

oval shape

red

black

navy blue

Use some paint to experiment with colours:

1. Choose a primary colour and add other colours to it.
2. Keep a record of the colours you mix together and the new colours they make.
3. Use the different colours you have made to paint something simple like sky or water.

How many colours do you think there are? 10? 20? 100? 1000? More?

sweet
wrapper

Now try this:
1. Collect see-through coloured sweet wrappers.
2. Tape some of the wrappers to a window and overlap them to make different colours.
3. Fold some wrappers in half to make stronger colours.

Colours working together

Decorated spinners.

When colours move, our eyes can see things which are not there. Spinning colours can have a strange effect. Make some simple spinners and decorate them. Use the **designs** shown here to help you.

You can make a spinner as follows:

1. Cut out a circle of card about 15 cm wide and ask an adult to make two holes about 1 cm from the centre.
2. Draw a design on one side and then colour it. Repeat the design on the other side but colour it differently.
3. Get some thin string or wool and thread it through the two holes. Knot the string to make a loop.

Hold the string in both hands, twist it and then gently pull. The card will spin and you will see the colours change.

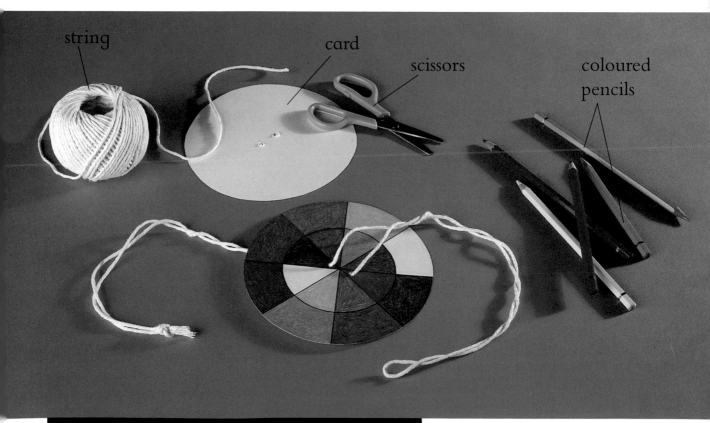

string   card   scissors   coloured pencils

You need these things to make a spinner.

Colours and tones

Adding white   Adding purple   Adding white   Adding green

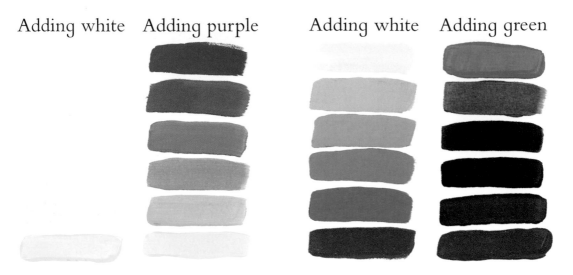

Adding white   Adding orange

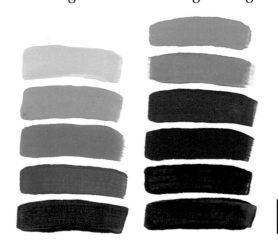

Tones that match each other on the ladders often work best together in paintings.

Different tone ladders.

Use paints to make tone ladders.
1. Put two big blobs of one of the primary colours onto a palette.
2. Add small amounts of white paint to one of the blobs.
3. Then add tiny amounts of the complementary colour to the other blob.
4. As you make different shades, add them to your tone ladder like the ones shown above.

Here Claude Monet has used the light and dark tones of purple, blue and green to paint his lily pond. Monet was interested in the way light and water **interacted** to keep changing the **scene**.

Monet painted his lily pond many times. Each picture is different.

blue

green

purple

waterlily

Claude Monet, *Waterlilies*, 1907.

Painting with dots

river bank

river

bather

Georges Pierre Seurat, *Bathers at Asnieres*, 1883-84.

Georges Seurat was an artist who **experimented** with colour in a **scientific** way. He used tiny dots of colour. Look at the boy on the right side of the picture. He seems surrounded with bright light. Seurat used light and dark **tones** and mixed them together to create this special effect.

Seurat's way of painting tricks us into seeing colours. The colours blend in our heads, not on the **canvas**! Try experimenting with tiny dots of coloured paint. Make a simple picture just using dots of colour – it is not as easy as it first looks!

Glossary

a
b
c
d
e
f
g
h
i
j
k
l
m
n
o
p
q
r
s
t
u
v
w
x
y
z

Aborigine   native person of Australia

abstract   kind of art which does not try to
                    show people or things, but instead
                    uses shape and colour to make the
                    picture

canvas   strong woven material on which
                    many artists paint

combination   two or more things together

complement   make another colour seem bright

complementary   a colour opposite another on
   colour   the colour wheel

contrasts   differences that you can see when
                    things are compared

decorative   pleasant or interesting to look at

design   lines and shapes which decorate art

earth colour   warm colour found in nature, such as
                    brown or red

experiment   try things out, or repeat something
                    until you like the result

explore   examine how something works

hieroglyphs	pictures used by the ancient Egyptians instead of words
interact	how things work with each other
monastery	building where monks live and pray
overlap	partly cover
palette	board used to mix colours on
primary colour	red, blue and yellow – colours which cannot be made by mixing other colours
secondary colour	colour which is made by mixing two primary colours together
scene	view painted by an artist
scientific	like science, testing ideas in an ordered way
shade	a darker or lighter version of a colour
stained glass	small pieces of coloured glass put together to make a picture
tone	shades and depth of colour, from light to dark or dull to bright

a
b
c
d
e
f
g
h
i
j
k
l
m
n
o
p
q
r
s
t
u
v
w
x
y
z

Index

Table of contents

Introduction to book-keeping

Most people who are in business for the first time wrongly believe that keeping a set of books is an unnecessary and unpleasant task, a chore they must undertake simply for the benefit of the taxman. It is true that the Inland Revenue will use the accounts produced from your business records to extract the maximum amount of tax they can. On the other hand, a skilled accountant will be able to use them to minimise the tax liability for you and your business.

Keeping an accurate detail of all your business transactions should never be classed as a job to be done only when you can fit it into your busy schedule. Your business paperwork needs to be updated daily because it is the gauge of the financial health of your business. It is no good moaning that time could be more profitably spent making sales, because if you sell goods or services at a loss due to poor accounting procedures, what is the point of being in business? Did you know that more businesses fail in their first year or two because of insufficient financial control than for any other reason?

What makes this book different from the many others published over the years on book-keeping? It is because a businessman, not a qualified accountant, has written it, and primarily for the entrepreneur. Whilst students and those entering book-keeping and accountancy careers for the first time will find it very helpful, it is not a textbook. It is really aimed at small business owners. Apart from showing how to set up accounting records and explaining the jargon used by those in the profession, it also demonstrates the practical uses to which a go-ahead businessperson can put the information stored within the accounts of a business.

Since the financial records of an owner-managed enterprise can differ greatly from those of medium-sized and larger businesses, Chapters 2 and 3 relate to the book-keeping requirements of a sole proprietor, for example, a self-employed tradesman or small shopkeeper, in fact anyone mainly trading in cash and not credit transactions. If you fall into this grouping, you will have little use for double entry book-keeping, and piles of ledgers. What you really need is an easy-to-operate, no-frills system and that's exactly what you get in these chapters. Nevertheless, it is important not to neglect some of the later chapters, as these will be invaluable to you as a source of reference; I refer to the segments on Balance Sheets, Profit and Loss Accounts, computerised accounting and payroll (even if only employing one member of staff).

At the end of each fiscal year, putting the final accounts together will be a lot easier for your accountant if he or she is presented with a full set of well-kept books, instead of simply giving him piles of invoices and receipts to sort out. Apart from ensuring you are not paying too much tax, his fees will be much less.

Those of you who are on the threshold of an exciting new business adventure may be interested in reading my other books in Law Pack's Made

Easy series, namely *Running Your Own Business Made Easy*, *Debt Collection Made Easy* and *Earning and Keeping Customer Loyalty Made Easy*. Each draws on personal experience in assisting you in avoiding the pitfalls I encountered when embarking on the same path you are now taking.

Finally, I would like to thank the many firms and individuals without whose help I would have been unable to write this book.

Roy Hedges

Book-keeping & accounting explained

1

Chapter 1

Book-keeping & accounting explained

What you'll find in this chapter:

- ➠ Different forms of accounting made clear
- ➠ Who keeps books and why?
- ➠ Assets, liabilities and capital
- ➠ Business transactions clarified

There are a number of organisations and people who will have an interest in the financial standing of your business, whether it is your customers paying what they owe you, or your backers wanting to know that your business is solvent and not about to collapse. Therefore, keeping an accurate record of all transactions as they occur will provide the financial history you and other interested parties require.

Before describing why other people and organisations seek financial information about your business, let's first look at the three distinct groupings they fall into, the initial grouping being the:

- Inland Revenue

- Customs and Excise

Naturally, these two require the information for taxation purposes. Corporation Tax, Income Tax, PAYE, Capital Gains Taxes and Inheritance Tax all fall into the domain of the Inland Revenue. Customs and Excise are concerned with import duties and VAT. Next there are:

> *note* The art of getting new money invested in a business relies on having a sound business plan. For that, you need a 'proper set of books'.

- Banks

- Finance houses

- Building societies

Your bank or account manager will certainly expect you to have proper financial controls in place if you are intending to arrange a loan or overdraft. The same rule applies if you are contemplating leasing cars or equipment; perhaps you may require a mortgage. Finally, the largest group includes:

- Investors

- Shareholders

- Customers (debtors)

- Suppliers (creditors)

- Management

- Companies House (limited companies are obliged to submit copies of their annual accounts to Companies House)

And, of course, there is you. You'll need to know on a day-to-day basis the value of your sales and purchases. Those considering investing in your business (including shareholders) will want to know that their money is reasonably safe. Customers, on the other hand, may need to be assured that your firm is sufficiently solvent to honour any guarantee or pledge you offer. Suppliers will want to be as certain as possible that any goods or services they sell you will be paid for, according to their terms of trade. As for management, they will be able to tell if their departments are on target - if not, they should be able to rectify the situation.

As you can see, having a basic understanding of book-keeping is important for all businesspeople; even if you employ a part-time book-keeper to make the actual entries in your accounts, you may be called upon to explain certain items recorded in your books to your bank manager. Many

> **note** Using accountants is fine for preparing end of year accounts. However, it is your business and you must always be in financial control.

firms and individuals could be interested in the financial strength of your business. From the beginning, not all those listed above will require financial information about your firm, but the list will grow as you expand.

Obviously, a sole trader working from home, such as a builder, carpet-layer or surveyor, does not need to keep a full set of books; a couple of simple books accompanied by two lever-arch files, one for payments and another for receipts and bank statements will suffice. This also applies to the sole trader running a small shop. We shall take a deeper look at this system of book-keeping and show you how it works a little later. A computer with easy-to-use spreadsheet software will do the same for you as a purchase book. There is a lot more detail to be found about computerised accounting in Chapter 6.

Businesses do not stand still. They either stagnate and die, or prosper and expand. As growth should be your ultimate aim, we will assume that eventually you would like to progress from sole trader to limited company. For this, you will need to be able to interpret the information in your accounts; a guide to this can be found in later chapters. Ensuring accurate financial data is constantly available is important if you require additional finance to develop your business, either by organic growth or by acquisition. If you do decide to sell at any time, a potential buyer of your business will need to ensure it is as good as you have stated.

note It is advisable for all sole traders to have two bank accounts, thus keeping trade and personal spending separate.

Different forms of accounting made clear

By and large, accounts for businesses fall into three distinct groups:

· Daily control of transactions including cash management

· Monthly or quarterly management accounts

· Annual accounts

Cash management, as its name implies, provides an insight into a business's ability to meet its financial obligations as they fall due. Cash flow forecasting, for example, falls into this category.

Although monthly or quarterly management accounting is the most important, in small businesses it tends to be ignored. These vital reports, when compared with previous predictions and forecasts, will confirm if your business is on track and not running at a loss. Leaving this until the year-end could mean you leave things too late.

Businesspeople need to understand book-keeping, if only to enable them to interpret their accounts fluently to prospective lenders.

Finally, the annual or final accounts are as important as the previous two. These provide a year-on-year analysis of the profitability or loss of your enterprise. They will also confirm whether your business has been running efficiently or not, over the longer term. It is from these annual reports that your income and tax can be assessed. Every one of these three accounting categories has an important role to play in your business.

Who keeps books and why?

The recording of all financial events in a set of accounts provides an accurate history of what has happened to a business in a given period. At the end of each fiscal year, the final accounts produced are only a mirror of the financial health of an enterprise at the time of the end of year report. Never assume that a business that was in profit at the time of its annual accounts is still profitable six months later.

The role of book-keeping and accounting in business is best summed up in the following manner. Book-keeping is the recording of business transactions, from the financial point of view, on a day-to-day basis. Accounting is the preparation of financial statements - a Balance Sheet which summarises the firm's assets and liabilities at a certain date and a Profit and Loss Account which shows how much the firm has made or lost in the period ending on the Balance Sheet date.

Accounts are made to achieve the following:

- To gather facts and figures from an accounting system in order to assist the entrepreneur in making vital decisions and predictions about the direction a business must take.

note Book-keeping has changed little from its inception, over five centuries ago. Only the methods of operation have altered.

- To classify such items as purchases, sales, expenses and bank balances, etc.

- To find out how much money is owed to suppliers and is owed by customers.

- To measure results, and in particular, to calculate profits and losses.

- To establish the liquidity of a business (as profit does not necessarily mean cash).

- To provide proper financial controls.

By law, large businesses are required to keep to strict accounting procedures and record all transactions accurately. Sole traders, on the other hand, do not have the same stringent rules placed upon them. Whilst small limited companies must also submit accounts to Companies House each year, the rules are a little more relaxed than those that apply to public limited companies.

It is all very well stating that it is important for every type of business to keep a set of accounts, but who will actually do the hard, and sometimes monotonous, work? Regarding a sole trader or small retailer and others in this category, there is only the owner or perhaps his or her spouse. As the business expands, a part-time book-keeper may be appropriate. Usually these small organisations have their final accounts prepared by a practising accountant, who will also be responsible for tax calculations, the preparation and completion of the final accounts, and at the same time for dealing with tax inspectors on behalf of their clients.

Large organisations employ their own personnel in-house to carry out these functions.

Accountants are usually members of one of the professional accounting bodies; they qualify by examination and practical experience.

> **TIP** Accountants in private practice may offer advice on accounting procedures, as well as providing payroll and other services - but at a price.

In larger organisations, there are three types of accountant:

Financial accountants prepare the statutory accounts that have to be filed at Company House. They also deal with most taxation matters.

Cost accountants analyse the costs of the components in the firm's products (including labour and overheads). They work out the price a manufacturer needs to charge for their products to maintain profitability.

Management accountants prepare budgets, forecasts and compare the actual performance against them.

All these accountants report to a financial director who co-ordinates the activities for these functions. Supporting the accountants are book-keepers, accounts clerks and accounting technicians. This group of staff enter the daily financial data into the books and ledgers. Attached to the accounts team and also reporting to the financial director is the credit manager, with his or her team of sales ledger clerks and credit controllers, plus the purchase ledger manager and ledger clerks.

Another set of accounting personnel not previously mentioned are the auditors of a business. These are accountants whose role it is to check that the accounting procedures are being followed correctly. Auditors fall into two distinct categories:

External auditors, as their title suggests, are completely independent of the firm whose accounts are being audited. The most common type of audit they undertake is the statutory audit of a

note Auditors, by the nature of their work, are required to act independently within a business, whether they are internal or external auditors.

limited company. Their main task is to provide a fair and unbiased report on a firm's assets and liabilities each year.

Internal auditors are employees of the business they audit. They are primarily concerned with checking the internal control procedures of the company.

> **TIP**
> As a general rule, external auditors report to a company's shareholders, whilst internal auditors, on the other hand, report to the firm's directors.

It could be said that entrepreneurs needn't bother with the practical workings of accounting functions, because they will be employing people to do that for them. In the early years, when building up businesses, I found that having the basic knowledge of accounting procedures ensured my businesses were always on the right track. Furthermore, I found that understanding a firm's accounts when buying a business was invaluable to me, particularly as I was able to confirm the reality of what a vendor told me before parting with hard-earned cash.

Assets, liabilities and capital

Before getting into the realm of actually setting up a book-keeping system for a sole trader, we need to take a short side-step to understand about the assets, liabilities and capital of a business, because these items are the same for every type of business, irrespective of size.

Assets are things a sole trader or business owns; they fall into two categories: current and fixed. Current assets are the firm's most 'liquid' type of asset; the most common form of current asset is cash either in hand or at the bank. It also can be such things as stock or debtors that can easily be

> *note* The very first book-keeping entry in most businesses is usually the transfer to the firm of the owner's capital.

converted into cash. Liquid assets are used by a business for its day-to-day operations. Fixed assets, on the other hand, are those retained by the firm or individual to carry on the business. Conventional fixed assets include land and buildings, plant and machinery, furniture and fittings and motor vehicles.

Liabilities fall into two main groups: current and long-term. Current liabilities refer to money owed by the business to suppliers, or wages and commission due to employees. It also includes bank overdrafts which are repayable on demand. Long-term liabilities cover items such as bank or finance house loans, private loans and mortgages; in fact, any formal loan or mortgage whose agreement requires some form of collateral security.

Capital is another form of liability. In so far as capital is the total amount of money invested by the owner(s) or shareholders, it is money owed by a business to the owner.

> *note* As a proprietor of a business, the owner is simply another creditor of the business.

It will be useful if you get into the practice of regarding a sole proprietor or shareholder as someone separate from the business. Whilst sole traders and their business are one and the same, it is better to consider them as separate entities in order to keep your personal finances and family life apart from the business. (Although when a business closes down the proprietor is the last person to be paid, because all creditors have to be paid before any capital can be refunded.)

Business transactions clarified

A business transaction is simply the transmission of goods or services and money from the seller to the buyer; whether it be purchasing groceries at the local supermarket or a multi-million-pound road construction project, they are still business transactions.

When a transaction involves the immediate payment for the supply of goods or services, it is a cash transaction. If payment is to be delayed, it is a credit transaction. It is of no importance whether payment is delayed a week or a month, or even years; the transaction will fall into the credit category.

note When credit is involved in a business deal, all that happens is an item of stock is turned into a debt; it becomes a completed transaction when payment is made.

A typical business's transaction will fall into two distinct actions:

1. The goods or services are supplied to the customer.

2. Payment is made, as per the terms of the transaction.

To summarise, keep a record of all these transactions by documenting the debts of a firm's customers, and the debts of the business to its suppliers. Also record all cash transactions in order to control the expenditure of a business.

Keeping records for the small business

2

Chapter 2

Keeping records for the small business

What you'll find in this chapter:	
⏩	The sales book
⏩	The cash book
⏩	The purchase book
⏩	The petty cash book
⏩	Using a credit card for business payments

Cash is king - we all know that - so it's vital that you monitor your cash flow accurately. The main advantages of having knowledge of book-keeping is that not only will it save you the expense of an accountant, but it can help you keep track of how your business is doing as you go along.

The last thing sole proprietors need is a complicated accounting system. What they really want is a simple, easy-to-operate method to keep track of (1) cash, (2) income and (3) expenditure. In order to provide more detail, I am going to describe keeping these records in three books but you can do it in one.

The cash book

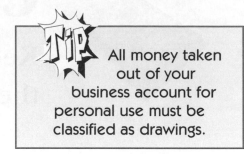

All money taken out of your business account for personal use must be classified as drawings.

This book monitors the movement of your money in and out of your bank account. From the first moment you begin trading, you will need to know how much cash is coming into your firm and how much is flowing out. Without this basic knowledge, you'll never know whether you have enough cash to pay your staff or suppliers.

The cash book monitoring your money should look like your bank statement; it will show you what cash is coming in and going out of your business, and what happens to it. Also, each month you must check that the bank doesn't make any errors, and with this method you can, simply by reconciling your cash book with your bank statement each month.

I recommend using a three-column cash book, as it allows you to keep a running balance of the cash you have available in the bank at any given moment in time. Without having to keep adding and subtracting figures, your actual balance can be seen at a glance. The reason for this is because invariably the balance at the bank or on your statement does not take into account cash or cheques in transit.

An example of the type of cash book recommended is shown below. All entries should show the date you actually sent a cheque to your supplier and details of the payee, including cheque number. The type of payment should be stated if you are not paying by cheque, for example, either by standing order (s/o) or direct debit (d/d).

Date	Description	Money in	Money out	Balance
Jan 2	Balance b/fwd			3,535.50
	Banked - Till Roll No 1 (less Contra £20)	352.28		3,887.78
	B. Smith C/Htg. Chq. No: 123		45.60	3,842.18
3	T. Knavish Gar. Chq. No: 124		53.84	3,788.34
	HH Finance d/d		250.00	3,538.34
	Banked - Till Roll No 2	529.85		4,068.19
4	Pensions R Us s/o - Drawings		125.00	3,943.19
	Banked Till Roll No 3	414.37		4,357.56
5	MC Ltd (Invoice 323)	28.40		4,385.96

A retailer's banking cash book

In this sample, I have assumed our retailer is a newsagent. In the course of business, the newsagent supplies a local company with trade magazines and newspapers for their reception area. As they prefer to pay monthly, he or she invoices them, hence in the last row reference is made to its number. This item would be recorded in the sales book as soon as it has been sent to the customer but obviously the cash can only be entered into the cash book once it has been received.

In this illustration a 'contra' item is shown; this is because not all the money received was banked. In this case, £20 was kept back to increase the daily float of loose change retained in the cash register, the petty cash. Had the item shown only reflected the actual amount banked; there would have been a deficiency between the cash received and cash at the bank. Contra entries save you having to bank the entire sales receipts and then write a cheque to withdraw the sum needed, requiring you to make additional entries in your books and pay extra bank charges into the bargain.

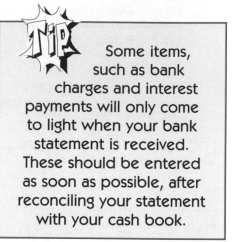

Some items, such as bank charges and interest payments will only come to light when your bank statement is received. These should be entered as soon as possible, after reconciling your statement with your cash book.

The date the payment is entered in your cash book and the date it actually leaves your account could vary considerably, depending on how long the payee takes to pay in your cheque.

Your cash book should reflect all transactions as and when they happen. If you only rely on your bank statement, it will not show those credits and debits that are in transit. The dates entered in your book should be the dates the cheque was made out or a deposit made. In the case of standing orders and direct debits, the date they are due to be paid should be used.

The sales book

I have found it easier to write up the books on a daily basis. If you do these things while they are fresh in your mind, there is less chance of errors occurring, and it only takes a couple of minutes a day.

This book will be used for recording your daily sales, or takings. For a shopkeeper, each day's takings will be entered in total. No one, not even the taxman, expects you to list individual sales. On the other hand, a decorator, for example, would only have one or two entries per week or month to record so more detail may be preferred.

For ease of reference, VAT has not been included in any illustration.

Week No: 1   **Commencing: 2 January 2002**

Date	Till roll no	Takings/sales Cash	Takings/sales Chq/Cr card	Totals
Mon 2/1	1	372.28		372.28
Tue 3/1	2	494.75	35.10	529.85
Weds 4/1	3	398.00	16.37	414.37
Thurs 5/1	4	254.86		254.86
Fri 6/1	5	529.44		529.44
Sat 7/1	6	783.56	103.40	886.96
Totals:		2,832.89	154.87	2,987.76

An average shopkeeper's sales book

As you can see, the totals of the cash and cheque columns across equal the total of the third column down. This method not only allows you to confirm your sums are right but it also ensures all amounts have been entered correctly and figures have not been transposed. Numbering every till roll will make it easy for your accountant to verify the amount of sales at the year-end. The till rolls can be filed in a folder or box file, once the entry has been made.

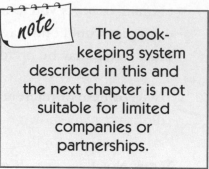

note

The book-keeping system described in this and the next chapter is not suitable for limited companies or partnerships.

Date	Detail	Amount	
Mon 2/1	Mr Jones, Any Rd, Newtown (Chq No 21)	952.18	
Thur 26/1	Smith's Stores, High St (Chq No 65)	421.50	
Tue 31/1	Monthly total		1,373.68

An example of a decorator's sales record

An extraordinary item such as an overdraft, loan or additional capital, would simply be entered under the weekly totals as: 'January 5 £5,000 Loan from Anytown Bank PLC', or capital introduced.

The purchase book

This book analyses the purchases in order to save paying an accountant to do the work. However, should you use a professional book-keeper, this book will be unnecessary.

If it is not your intention to use an accountant, the Inland Revenue can provide a large range of booklets to help you.

When analysing payments, the first two columns will show the date and description as shown before in the cash book example. To the right of these two columns will be a series of other columns, each one with a heading denoting the type of expense to which the payment relates. The number of columns you use will depend on the

note
To ensure you are using the correct headings in your expense columns, copy those listed in the Inland Revenue's self-assessment form supplied by your Tax Office.

type of business you are in. Also there is no set rule on how you classify your expenses. Some people prefer to keep utilities separate and have one column for electricity, and another for gas. Others may prefer to put these two items into a single column.

In the example of a purchase book below, you will note that apart from the name of the supplier in the item column, the method of payment is also shown. This helps you to reconcile your bank account and cash book. It should also be noted that the payment to G. Smith's Garage shows payments in two columns: this is because one cheque was used to pay for two expenses, one for private petrol purchased and the other for business. The two items are added together in the total column.

At the end of each page, and month, each column is totalled, and the sum of the totals along the bottom line must tally with the total at the bottom of the total column; thereby confirming every entry is correct.

Date	Item	Stationery	Drawings	Vehicles	Stock	Heating	HP/Loans	Rent	Total
4 Feb	G Smith Garage Chq No:84		20.00	53.84					73.84
	R & S Stationery Chq No: 85	189.15							189.15
5 Feb	M White C/H Ltd					45.60			45.60
	Roberts Finance (D/Debit)						250.00		250.00
	WA Estates Chq No:86							1,200.00	1,200.00
18 Feb	R & S Stationery Chq No:87	16.20							16.20
Totals		205.35	20.00	53.84		45.60	250.00	1,200.00	1,774.79

A purchase book

The analysis of the expenses in the purchase book enables you to see at a glance what costs you are incurring and makes the accountants job at the year-end easier - and cheaper.

There are a number of classifications that can be used to analyse expenditure; some of the most common are listed here, together with a general explanation of the differing items that can fall into each category.

Costs of sales (stock): Those goods you buy for resale to your customers. Or in a manufacturing business raw materials used in production of finished articles.

Employee costs: These include salaries and commissions, and sub-contractors expenses. Money paid to you is drawings and must not be included in this column, but wages paid to your spouse or partner would.

Premises: In this column you would include such things as insurance, rent and rates. If you are a small user, you could include heat and light. It is possible for those working from home to make an adjustment to offset part of your home expenses against business costs. An accountant will advise you on the proportion you are allowed to claim.

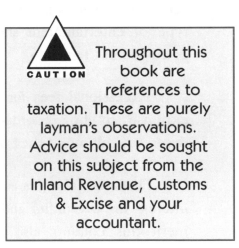

CAUTION Throughout this book are references to taxation. These are purely layman's observations. Advice should be sought on this subject from the Inland Revenue, Customs & Excise and your accountant.

Repairs include machinery used in your business, but not cars. Repairs to business property is an allowable expense, but not improvements. There can be a fine line between repairs and improvements; either read the Inland Revenue guidelines or see your accountant.

Administrative expenses cover a wide range. More items will end up in this column than anywhere else. Things such as telephone, postage, tea and coffee are just a few possibilities. Subscriptions to trade associations also fall into this category.

Travel and overnight accommodation fit into this classification, for business trips away from your area. Meals are also permissible if staying away overnight.

Vehicle expenses such as car repair, servicing and petrol costs fit into this sector. Also, a road fund licence can be included, but not fines for speeding or other motoring offences.

Advertising includes all promotional material, for example, for direct mail or newspaper advertising. Taking clients or suppliers to lunch is not a claimable business expense for taxation purposes. Notes of the cost of this type of entertainment should be included in your budgeting, which is discussed in Chapter 6.

Professional fees for accountants and solicitors, are another item of expense to be recorded and deserve a column of their own.

Financial charges such as interest on overdrafts and loans merit this column; also in this category would be leased equipment, but not cars, as they would fit into the vehicle list.

> *note* Some of the expense headings used here may not be applicable to your business, so just leave them out. However, there may be some headings not included, so simply add them to the list. The suggestions mentioned are not set in stone.

Columns for drawings should encompass anything of a personal nature, rather than a business expense.

You should have a column for each category of genuine business expenses. Nevertheless, there are some expenses, which in practice are borderline cases insomuch as they are part private and part business, petrol for example. As a general rule, your accountant should be able to negotiate with the Inland Revenue to apportion these types of costs.

Don't forget to claim for membership of trade and professional organisations.

What are allowable or disallowable business expenses is a minefield, and before setting out your columns you should read the Inland Revenue leaflet mentioned on page 23 and discuss it with your accountant. A few more allowable expenses are mentioned in the last chapter.

Dealing with petty cash

Inevitably there are times for every business, irrespective of its size, to make a cash purchase. In some firms, a simple metal cash box is used to keep the money safe, or in retail business the purchase may be made straight from the till. In either case, a record of the transaction must be kept.

Using a cash box normally requires a fixed sum of money being withdrawn from the bank and topped-up at regular intervals. The method of entry in the cash book and cheque stub will be no different from any other transaction.

Petty cash voucher	no 54		
	Date ___February 5_____		
		£	p
25 envelopes		1	12
2 pens			65
12 first class stamps		3	24
		5	01
Signature_____	Authorised by_____		

A typical petty cash voucher

There is no reason to purchase pads of petty cash vouchers; an odd scrap of paper will do. The important thing to remember is to complete a petty cash record as soon as the purchase is made or when you return to your shop or home. Otherwise, it could be forgotten, and you'll end up not claiming for it.

If you are using cash direct from the till, when it comes to banking the daily takings, a contra entry will be necessary. In both cases, a note or petty cash voucher is required to replace the money used. You will attach the receipt given at the time of purchase to the voucher.

One of the best systems for dealing with petty cash is the imprest method. This works as follows. Say you start off your petty cash with £50. During the course of a week you take from the cash box enough money to pay for fares, cleaning materials, tea and coffee.

note The advantage of this method is that petty cash can be checked for accuracy at short notice and at regular intervals.

Each time you spend a sum of money, a petty cash voucher replaces the cash spent. At the end of the week, every voucher is added together with the remaining cash and the total should be £50. Now if your purchases came to £40, for example, your petty cash is reimbursed by this sum to start you off on the following week with £50 again, thus restoring the imprest position. In larger organisations the petty cash voucher would be signed by a manager; in a small business it would be initialled by the owner - this would vouch for the authenticity of the expense. Numbering the vouchers allows them to be filed in numerical order, making it easier for your accountant when auditing the books at year-end. It also helps to identify the payment when your firm's expenses are being analysed at the end of the week or month. The imprest system can be, and is, used by all businesses irrespective of their size.

The petty cash book

The petty cash book analyses expenses in the same way as the purchase book. All you need is a simple analysis sheet and at the end of each month put the petty cash vouchers in order, all travel dockets in one pile, and stationery items in another and so forth. Total each pile and record the totals on an analysis sheet.

Date	Cash from bank/contra	Cheque Numbers	Total Expenses	Travel	Stationery	Cash balance
Jan	Petty cash	128	40.00	15.00	12.50	2.50

A simple petty cash analysis sheet

Using credit cards for business payments

Credit cards are being increasingly used to pay for business expenses. Some credit card companies will issue a second card, or set up another account solely for business purposes. You are advised, for the same reason as having separate bank accounts, to have two credit card accounts, one for business and the other for private use. Another reason for having separate card accounts is that if you do not pay the card balance in full each month, you will be unable to claim tax relief on the interest as a business expense.

Always remember to include the charges card processors make, and the interest element if not paying the account in full each month, with other financial costs as an expense. Credit card statements should be filed as any other receipt or invoice.

Because of the steep interest charges, it is always advisable to pay the credit card bill in full each month and not take advantage of the credit facility. Not only are there cheaper finance deals available but it can also cause complications when recording transactions. Paying for an item by credit card is no different from paying by cheque - you have incurred the expense on the day you sign the voucher. If you do make numerous credit card transactions, I recommend that you create a credit card book to analyse this expenditure.

Reconciliation & VAT

Chapter 3

Reconciliation and VAT

What you'll find in this chapter:

▦➡ Business bank accounts

▦➡ Reconciling your accounts

▦➡ What to do at the end of the year

▦➡ Value Added Tax

Business bank accounts

In Chapter 1 you were advised to maintain two bank accounts, one for your business and a personal one. The reasoning behind this suggestion was to keep private expenditure separate from the day-to-day business expenses.

This also allows you to keep a true record of pure business transactions, and avoids the problems associated with the self-employed using money in the till or sales income as their own.

Having a separate bank account provides independent evidence of the income and expenditure of the business for the Inland Revenue, and the risk of paying too much tax is reduced. It also will be easier to check the business records against the bank statement each month.

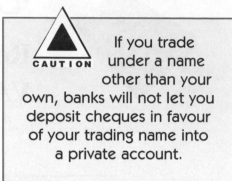

If you trade under a name other than your own, banks will not let you deposit cheques in favour of your trading name into a private account.

Depending on the size of your business, it is advisable to check your bank statement daily online and enter all transactions in the cash book. At month-end, you will then draw a line under all the books and total the figures so you can start the new month with a clean sheet.

Reconciling your accounts

Here we are talking about reconciling your cash book with your bank statement. It is important that all cheque and paying-in book stubs have enough information on them so that they are easily identifiable. On receipt of your statement from the bank each month, you need to check that every cheque has been cleared. To do this, simply match the entry in your cash book and the corresponding cheque stub with your statement. Tick each item that has been cleared. As you go down your statement, you may find some items have not been cleared. The same may apply to a deposit made late in the month. All you need to do to ensure your balance corresponds

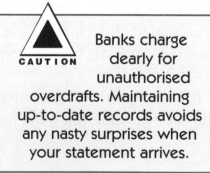

Banks charge dearly for unauthorised overdrafts. Maintaining up-to-date records avoids any nasty surprises when your statement arrives.

with the bank is list all unpaid items and deduct their total from the bank's balance, and with the credit items not shown add these to the balance. The balance in your cash book should now coincide with the figures on the statement; if it doesn't, you have an error somewhere.

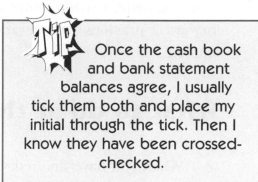

Once the cash book and bank statement balances agree, I usually tick them both and place my initial through the tick. Then I know they have been crossed-checked.

As you check through your statement, you may come across certain items such as interest charges, or an electronic payment not shown in your cash book. Before reconciling your balances, make sure that you enter these items into your cash book, and that they are transferred to the purchase book.

As you will be making the entries in the cash book as you go along, some of the early transactions on the statement might not be listed in the current cash book, because the transaction took place in the previous month. All you have to do is go back to the previous month's cash book entries and tick the offending item to confirm that it has now cleared.

When your accounts have been reconciled, don't just put them away and forget them. Later you will be shown how to use this information to your advantage.

Errors will naturally occur from time to time; more often than not, they are a simple mathematical discrepancy. Quickly readding your figures should solve the problem. If not, by subtracting the two totals from the resulting sum, if it is only one mistake, will point you to the omission. It could be that you just omitted to enter a contra amount. Usually errors are simple mistakes, like forgetting to bring forward a previous balance and are quickly rectified; but they cannot be ignored.

What to do at the end of year

When you have finished writing up your books and analysed them on the last trading month of your financial year, all you need to do is then hand them all over to your accountant, together with all invoices and receipts.

The first thing accountants will do is to get their book-keeper to put all the month-end totals onto another analysed sheet to get the year's totals. If you do this before handing over your books, it will not only save you some money, it will also provide you with a detailed statement of your expenses. This will come in very handy when we cover budgeting and cash flow forecasting in Chapter 6.

Using the next page of your purchase book, set the columns across with the same headings that you had each month. In the rows down, forget the date column and in the item column put each month. In the remaining columns put the corresponding totals under each heading. After the twelfth month, have a total row and add them all up to obtain your year's totals, as per the short example shown below:

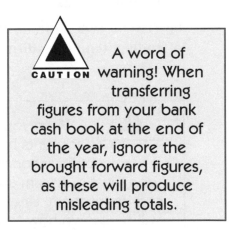

A word of warning! When transferring figures from your bank cash book at the end of the year, ignore the brought forward figures, as these will produce misleading totals.

	Stationery	Drawings	Vehicles	Total
January	360.00	750.00	545.00	1,655.00
February	75.00	750.00	367.00	1,192.00
Totals	435.00	1,500.00	912.00	2,847.00

It is very easy for errors to occur when transferring the figures, so please take extra care. For most small cash businesses working from home, there will be little else to do. Unfortunately, a retailer will have some adjustments to make. Not all the stock purchased by a retailer will have been sold at the end of the year, so an adjustment to his or her payments will have to be made. For simplicity, let's assume our shopkeeper buys for resale 50 bars of chocolate at £1 each and sells 20 of them for £1.50 each. A profit of £10 is made and there are 30 bars of chocolate remaining for the retailer to sell next year. So underneath the column for cost of sales the retailer must include £30 to get at the true sales and profits figures. As this adjustment really relates to stock and a shopkeeper will have more than one item of stock in the shop at the end of the year, it would be prudent to undertake a stocktake.

Stocktaking is counting the actual stock remaining at the year-end and valuing it. A written list of stock together with its cost of purchase is all that is required to satisfy the Inland Revenue. It is greatly different in manufacturing businesses, and this is dealt with in a little more detail in Chapter 5.

> **note** Service industries do not have stock as such, but they may have carried out work yet to be invoiced. This results in an adjustment to income being made.

Value Added Tax

This book is not intended as a tax guide, but as a businessperson you may have to account for this tax within your book-keeping system at some time in your business life. At present the basic rate of tax is 17.5 per cent. This rate applies to most business transactions. There is also a five per cent rate, which applies to utilities such as gas and water suppliers, and to certain property conversion work. There is also a zero rate which is dealt with below. Whilst the rate of 17.5 per cent has remained at this figure for some time, the Chancellor of the Exchequer has the power to raise or lower the rate in his annual budgets. Since this tax is added at every stage of production, anyone buying goods for resale or to use in their business pays tax on the goods purchased. For VAT, the collecting authority is HM Customs and Excise, not the Inland Revenue.

The VAT on goods or services you buy is called Input Tax. When charging your customers for the goods or services you supply to them, you add the appropriate rate of VAT - this levy is called the Output Tax.

Unsurprisingly, this Output Tax has to be handed over to the collecting authority's VAT department. But before doing so, the trader is allowed to deduct the amount of Input Tax paid at the time of purchasing the goods or raw materials. As the Output Tax is generally greater than the Input Tax, the business only pays the difference. The VAT formula is Output Tax - Input Tax = Amount payable to HM Customs.

There are some goods, namely food, books and children's clothing, that are zero-rated for VAT. A grocer, for example, would not charge customers VAT on the food they bought, but would be paying tax on the equipment bought for use in the shop, such as paper bags. Therefore, a grocer selling purely food items would be paying Input Tax on some purchases, and not receiving any Output Taxes on his or her sales. As a result, this type of business would be entitled to a refund from the collecting authority.

Finding out which goods are zero-rated, and which are not, is vital for some retailers. Although food is zcro-rated, confectionery is taxed at the standard rate. When it comes to exempt goods, or if the business produces partially rated and exempt goods, the rules

> **note** Customs and Excise offer a free comprehensive VAT guide [Leaflet Number 700], which will answer many of the teething troubles you may come across.

become very complicated indeed. Expert advice should be sought if you fall into this category.

As far as invoices are concerned, VAT must be shown in the United Kingdom by all VAT registered businesses, thus making it a tax invoice. All tax invoices and receipts must be recorded in your accounting system, and retained for inspection by HM Customs and Excise for a period of six years. If our grocer sells other non-food items, the VAT may equal out, with no payment due to or from HM Customs.

It is mandatory to register for VAT purposes once your turnover reaches a preset figure. This is referred to as the registration limit; as this limit generally increases each year in line with inflation, there is little point in quoting the current limit - a word with your accountant or local VAT office will provide this amount for you. It is also possible to register for VAT purposes before reaching the statutory limit if you consider your turnover will exceed the limit within the current financial year. Also, because of the nature of your business, if the Input Tax is constantly greater than the Output Tax and your business is below the threshold limit, it is possible to register for VAT, allowing you to claim the refunds.

One point you must consider when making an application for registration if trading below the statutory limit is that you will be required to charge all your customers VAT for the goods or services they buy from you. This could remove any trading advantage you may have over your competitors.

> **note**
>
> VAT is paid to HM Customs & Excise every three months, whilst tax refunds are paid monthly.

The recent introduction of the flat-rate scheme of VAT for small businesses with a turnover below a certain pre-set level, which is assumed will vary annually, goes some way to relieving the small businessperson from the administrative burden of calculating VAT payments.

What HM Customs and Excise have done is to set a rate of VAT for each business sector, which you may opt to pay instead of following the procedures mentioned above. It is important to bear in mind that your circumstances will determine whether opting for the flat-rate scheme will actually benefit you or not. Only by comparing the amount of VAT paid in previous years will you know if using the new scheme will be to your advantage.

The downside of this new flat-rate VAT scheme is that unless you maintain sufficient records you will be unaware if you are over- or underpaying VAT. The fear of overpayment may make this scheme unacceptable to many small businesses.

Before making any registration for VAT, it is a wise precaution to discuss this matter with your accountant, or local VAT office. Either of these two will spell out your responsibilities and liabilities clearly.

Accounting for VAT on taxable supplies is not as tricky as it may first seem. The main point to remember is that you are acting as a tax collector for HM Customs and Excise. The money does not belong to the business and therefore should not be treated as income. It is money in transit, which needs to be kept separate from the money in your business, until it is time to complete the VAT form and send it to the collecting authority. I have always found when running a small business that opening a saving account with the money waiting to be paid to HM Customs and Excise at the end of the accounting period provides a little extra revenue. To account for VAT, all you need to do is add another column to your sales book, as the diagram below shows.

Date	Till Roll	Takings/sales Cash	Taking/sales Chq/Cr.card	Totals Banked	VAT
Wed 4/1	3	398.00	16.37	414.37	72.51

A shopkeeper's sales book

The takings columns will show the net sales figure after deducting the VAT element in a retail shop where customers are not invoiced directly, but VAT has been included in the sale price. In the above example, the actual money received during the course of the day was £486.88. As the VAT is not part of the shop's takings, the retailer deducts 7/47ths from the total cash received to arrive at the net sales figure. The same rule applies to your purchases.

At the end of the quarter, when you have to complete the VAT return, you simply add the VAT columns in your sales and purchase books and deduct the input and output totals from each other. When the outputs are greater than the inputs, this is the sum you must pay to HM Customs and Excise VAT Department.

Listed here are a few other items, which are borderline cases when deciding if VAT is to be levied or not. Although you will receive a booklet from HM Customs when you register, giving you full details, it is advisable to be aware that such dilemmas exist.

- Bank charges are exempt, as are road fund licences.

- Leasing contracts carry VAT, but hire purchase agreements don't.

- Books for reading are zero-rated, but books you fill in, such as account books, carry a standard rating.

One major VAT problem businesspeople constantly face is vehicles. If you use a van exclusively for business travel, there is no problem with reclaiming VAT on fuel. However, if you use a car for business and private travel, you will have to prove to the VAT department what percentage of the mileage is business use and what is private. Guidelines are provided when you first register.

CAUTION You cannot claim back the VAT on goods purchased for personal consumption, only those used solely in your business.

One advantage of being registered for VAT is that if you are trading in a business-to-business environment your customers will not be bothered about you charging them VAT because they will simply claim it back. It's your prices before you add this levy that they are worried about.

Another advantage you have is that VAT is only collected quarterly, and as you have another four weeks in which to pay, you effectively have a permanent interest free loan from the taxman. That can't be bad, especially if it's earning you interest. Small businesses, such as builders or decorators with a turnover below the compulsory registration limit, have the advantage of lower prices when dealing with the end user, over those who have to charge VAT for their services.

Accounting for growing businesses

4

Chapter 4

Accounting for growing businesses

What you'll find in this chapter:

➡ Ledgers and accounts

➡ Daybooks

➡ Managing original documents

➡ Purchase and sale ledgers

When is the best time to begin thinking about using a more complicated method of keeping financial records? This would be when the number of financial transactions in your business has risen to such a level that you need to employ a book-keeper, at least on a part-time basis. Most businesspeople, when they reach this stage, are usually only too eager to pass their book-keeping duties onto someone else, leaving everything to the book-keeper they employ. Dont make this mistake! It is your business and only you must be in full financial control of it, not your book-keeper or accountant.

note If you own a business where the number of transactions is too small to use the double entry system, skip this and the next chapter and revisit them once your business has expanded.

Don't worry! This and the next chapter will provide you with a summary sufficient for you to be knowledgeable on the subject, without being an expert. If you understand the basic fundamental principles of double entry book-keeping, you will be able to interpret and comprehend your final accounts, as well as knowing how your business is doing. With this information at your fingertips, you will also be in a position to make sound business decisions and forecasts. Later on you may wish to buy another business, and of course, you will want to know if it is financially healthy. Furthermore, an understanding of this subject will be invaluable when interviewing accounts staff.

A point to bear in mind when upgrading your accounts procedures through expansion is that it might make sense to change from a manual to a computerised system at the same time. For more information on computerised accounting, see Chapter 6.

TIP Maintaining the regular upkeep of your books of account, will help to prevent your enterprise from failing.

Ledgers and accounts

Accounts are used to record the change of assets and liabilities on a day-to-day basis. So when you spend money or sell stock, entries are made in the appropriate account. An expenditure of cash will be recorded in the Cash Account, for example. The loss occurred when a debtor goes bust will be recorded in the Bad Debt Account, and so on.

The first transaction that takes place when someone starts a new business is the record of cash from its owner to the business. The entries for this transaction can be seen below. The double entry system requires the transaction to be recorded twice, once as a debit entry in the Cash Account, and another as a credit one in the Capital Account. This is known as the fundamental accounting equation. After the cash injection, the business owns the asset of £10,000 in cash, but owes the same amount to the providers of capital. You will note that each account has an account number in the top right-hand corner.

	CASH ACCOUNT							L1.
Dr.								Cr.
2002			£					
2 Jan	Capital	L2	10,000					

	CAPITAL ACCOUNT - Ted Knavish							L2.
Dr.								Cr.
				2002			£	
				2 Jan	Cash	L2	10,000	

You will observe from these specimen accounts that the page is divided in the centre, the left-hand side is named the debit side, and the right-hand side becomes the credit side. In most firms 'Dr' and 'Cr' are used as abbreviations.

When Mr. Knavish paid his money into his business, it was because he needed to buy equipment, pay the rent on his premises and buy some stock for resale. Whilst the Capital Account L2 remains unaltered, the Cash Account will now look like this:

CASH ACCOUNT							L1.
Dr.							
2002			£	2002			£
2 Jan	Capital	L2	10,000	2 Jan	Equipment	L3	2,500
					Rent	L4	750
					Stock	L5	4,250
					Balance c/d		2,500
			10,000				10,000
1 Feb	Balance b/d		2,500				

At this point the business still owes £10,000 to the providers of capital, but its assets are now worth £9,250. The difference between the value of the assets and liabilities is £750, the rent expense. A Balance Sheet drawn up at this point will show the £750 as an accumulated loss deducted from the capital.

Three further accounts will need to be opened. They will be numbered L3, L4, and L5 respectfully.

Accounts are normally grouped into three ledgers:

The sales ledger, or debtors' ledger, as it is sometimes called. This keeps a record of all the people that owe your business money. This means a customer whom you have sold goods or services to on credit.

> *note*
>
> Every transaction that takes place in a business involves a change in either the assets or liabilities of that business.

Purchase ledger, or creditors' ledger. These are the people to whom you owe money - your suppliers. This and the sales ledger are covered in a little more detail later in this chapter.

Nominal ledger which includes all the other accounts, whether Balance Sheet items (assets and liabilities) or Profit and Loss items (revenues and costs).

Daybooks

For every transaction that takes place in your business, whether it is a sale, return, purchase or a payment, or any other type of transaction, there has to be an original document, such as an invoice, credit note or petty cash voucher.

Daybooks are classed as books of prime entry because they are the first place in a business where transactions are recorded, like the purchase and sales books described earlier. When you receive a document, it is first recorded in a daybook and then you post the transaction details from the daybook to a ledger. There may come a time when your business grows to such an extent that one person alone cannot handle all the book-keeping entries. When this occurs, it is not possible for more than one person to work on a firm's daybook at a time, so it's divided into five subsidiary books, which are as follows:

> *note*
>
> Letters of complaint can be classed as original documents for the purpose of book-keeping, and as such they must be recorded and urgent action taken; simply because they can delay an account being paid, thus affecting the cash flow of a business.

- The purchase daybook - which records purchases.

- The sales daybook - where all sales are recorded.

- The purchase returns book - in which all returns outwards are noted.

- The sales return book - for recording returns inwards.

- The journal proper - any other transactions.

It should be noted that computerisation of accounts have largely rendered these five books extinct, now only to be found where manual book-keeping systems are in operation.

Managing original documents

When a firm buys goods, it is given an invoice. The same applies when you sell your products or services; you supply the buyer with an invoice. It documents the deal. That invoice, irrespective of whether you are giving or receiving it, becomes part of your contract for the sale of goods. It is evidence that can be used in a court of law, should a dispute arise. An invoice must contain the following information:

- Name and address of both buyer and seller.

- The date of the transaction.

- Description of the goods or services.

- Quantity, unit price and details of any discounts offered.

- The amount of VAT charged if any.

- Terms of trade of the seller, particularly the terms of credit if applicable and details of any discount awarded for prompt payment.

The invoice usually has two copies: the top copy is handed or posted to your customer, and the second is used to enter the transaction in your books. Now there are two variations of the invoice. One becomes a delivery note; the other an advice note which is usually contained in the parcel to be delivered. The advice note allows the buyer to check that the number, colour and size of the goods ordered is correct. Your driver uses the delivery note to confirm that delivery has been made, by getting the buyer to sign it. Invoices, as with any other document, must be retained for six years in accordance with the Limitation Act of 1980.

If there is a shortage between the number of items ordered and the amount delivered, the seller raises a credit note. The same applies if one or more of the items delivered is damaged. This document appears in the same format as the invoice, but with the words 'credit note replacing invoice'. Credit notes save the buyer from paying the full invoice value and receiving payment for the error. Credit notes are also issued when a mistake takes place in calculating the invoice totals, or the wrong price is quoted. Debit notes can be issued to the purchaser to indicate to the seller that a mistake has happened and that they require a refund.

TIP To ensure there is no misunderstanding regarding when you expect to be paid, always state your terms of trade clearly on all documents sent to your customers.

The seller will also issue monthly statements of account, unpaid invoices and the balance due for payment.

It is advisable to attach a remittance advice to your statements to assist in prompt payment. In fact, anything you can do to assist your customers to pay on time will help to ease your cash flow.

Many companies issue a purchase order, as do all local and central government offices when purchasing goods or services. This specifies the type of goods required, the number, colour, etc. It may also quote any agreed price that was negotiated. Purchase orders invariably quote a purchase or order number. Unless this number is quoted on all your documents, particularly invoices, payment can be delayed. This rule also applies when chasing up late payment.

Original documents should be stored securely in fireproof cabinets. HM Customs and Excise and the Inland Revenue can also call upon them if they feel an investigation is necessary. Furthermore, customers tend to lose them, or pretend they are lost to delay payment. If they are safe and handy, copies can be quickly sent to them.

Purchase and sales ledgers

Let us begin with the purchase ledger. Buyers and purchase ledger managers in larger firms must ensure suppliers are creditworthy before confirming valuable orders. It does not matter if the goods being purchased are part of your ongoing manufacturing process or if they are being retailed to the end user; you need to be assured that your chosen supplier is reliable, i.e. they will deliver what you want, when you want it, at the price and specifications agreed. In smaller or medium-sized businesses not employing purchasing personnel, it is your duty as the owner/manager, or senior director, to ensure these criteria are met. Failure could mean your money is tied up in half-finished products. Or where the items are required for resale, a loss of your customer's confidence in your business could be the result.

On receipt of the seller's documents, apart from checking that the goods ordered have been delivered in their entirety and that there are no breakages, it is important to confirm that the invoice is accurate, and the price charged is correct. Sometimes the VAT, and any discounts to which you were entitled, may not have been calculated correctly. The time to check these matters is at the time of delivery, not when you are being chased for late payment.

When you receive the supplier's invoice, you enter the details into the purchase book. From here your book-keeper then credits the supplier's personal account, because they have given you the goods. Next you debit your purchase account and at the same time debit the VAT account with the VAT element of the invoice. In posting the transaction ('posting' is the term used by accounting staff for the action being taken), the accounts will look like this:

	T. Knavish		CL1
	5 Jan	PDB1	616.26

Purchases Account			GL14
31 Jan	Sundry creditors		
	PDB1	524.48	

VAT Account			GL15
31 Jan	Sundry creditors		
	PDB1	91.78	

Now let's look at the sales ledger, and its personnel and their credit control colleagues. The responsibilities of your sales ledger, and credit control managers are the exact opposite of those people looking after your bought or purchase ledger. It is as important for your sales ledger staff to know as much about your customers as anyone else in your organisation. It is vital that invoices and credit notes are issued in sufficient time to meet your customers' cut-off dates, ensuring your cash flow targets are met. Any request for credit notes must be investigated thoroughly, and if you confirm errors have been made, the credit note must be sent by first-class post to avoid a delay in

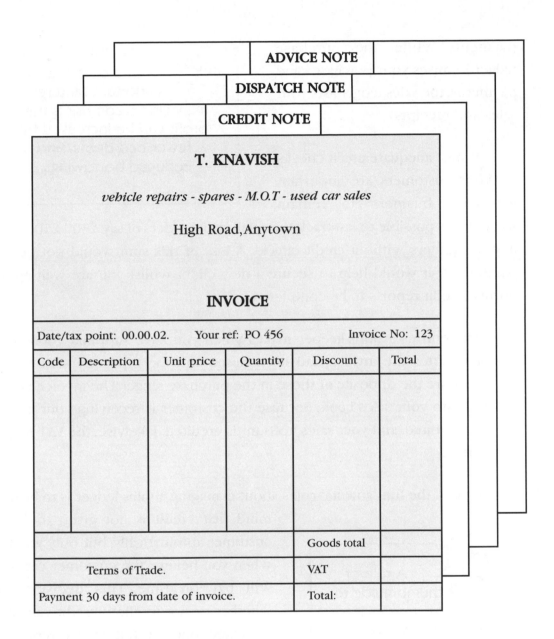

Samples of original documents

payment. While the purchase ledger itemises your purchases and payments, the sales ledger lists your sales and receipts.

> **note**
> One of the most important features of managing credit risk is that profit can be increased by fewer bad debts, and reduced borrowings.

Whilst adequate credit checks on your customers are important for your business to remain solvent, it is possible to fast-track the small initial orders of say £300–£500 from new customers without credit checks. A loss of this sum would not be too painful, but it would help to secure a new client whilst you are waiting for normal credit reports to be completed.

The entries a book-keeper makes when you have supplied goods to a customer, after the invoice had been raised and the top copy sent to the customer, are the opposite of those in the purchase ledger. The invoice is first entered into your sales book. Because the customer is receiving your goods, they are debited, and your sales account is credited. Likewise, the VAT ledger is credited.

One of the fundamental rules about managing a sales ledger is to bear in mind that credit is not given to every customer automatically, but only granted when you believe the customer can and will pay on time. This decision, on whether or not to allow credit can only be made once a full status report is received. A good credit manager knows that confirming the creditworthiness of customers increases sales, because your

> **TIP**
> A rule of thumb guide to ledger entries is to debit the receiver of the goods, and credit the giver.

sales team's efforts can be intensified with financially sound clients, instead of wasting their valuable time with a large number of poor-paying customers. You should never sell and hope to be paid, but build bridges with your customers and you will be paid on time and you will both have a long and profitable relationship.

Loyal customers turn small businesses into big ones.

Finally, what your sales ledger people should be doing whilst your bought ledger staff are avoiding interest being added to your cost, is ensuring any interest due is charged to your late paying customers.

Final accounts

Chapter 5
Final accounts

What you'll find in this chapter:

➡ Trial balances

➡ The Balance Sheet

➡ Stock valuation

➡ Trading and Manufacturing Accounts

➡ Profit and Loss Accounts

➡ Adjustments to the accounts

➡ Accounts of limited companies

➡ Year on year consistency in accounts

Trial balances

Before preparing the Profit and Loss Account and the Balance Sheet, your book-keeper will first draw up a trial balance. This is a list of all the accounts showing their closing balances. The total debits should equal the closing credits. If not, a mistake has been made and must be found. Trial balances are not only done at the end of each year, but can be taken at any time. If your accounts are computerised, a trial balance can be produced at the click of a button.

Every book-keeper should be able to account to trial balance; but at the year-end your auditors need to step in and finalise your books. Trying to get anyone else to do them is a false economy. Having said that, it is important that you understand what is involved in their preparation and how the information stored within them can be used.

> **note** A trial balance does exactly want its name implies - it confirms that the totals of the debit and credit entries match each other.

By doing a trial balance on a monthly basis, any slip made by your book-keeper in the month's work can be quickly spotted and rectified. Only doing it once a year could mean hours spent wading through months of paperwork.

The Balance Sheet

The Balance Sheet is just a reorganisation of the trial balance within a prescribed format. The Profit and Loss Account is merely a detailed breakdown of the profits figure shown below under 'Capital'.

Balance Sheet

As at 31 December 2002

Fixed assets	£	£	Capital	£	£
Premises		45,000.00	At start		50,000.00
Plant & machinery		110,000.00			
Office furniture		5,000.00	Profits	43,900.00	
		61,000.00	Drawings	10,400.00	

Current assets	£	£	Capital	£	£
					33,500.00
Stock	10,500.00				83,500.00
Sundry debtors	8,750.00				
Cash at bank	3,250.00				
Cash in hand	1,500.00		Long term liabilities		nil
			Current liabilities		
		24,000.00	Sundry creditors		1,500.00
		85,000.00			85,000.00

Stock valuation

Valuing stock correctly at the end of your trading year is important since it will reflect in your gross profits. Overvaluing it it could result in you paying too much tax. Undervaluing it could turn a profit into a loss, and this will reflect in your purchase price should you decide to sell the business. Because stock is shown in the Balance Sheet, an incorrect valuation could be looked upon as fraudulent, so care must be exercised at all times.

 When valuing stock, always price it at its cost price, reducing the value where deterioration has occurred.

In most businesses, it is advisable to keep a running total of stock in hand. This means every year you start off with an opening number of items in stock. During the course of the year this stock will be replenished; at the same time items of stock will either be used in your manufacturing process or sold. Stock items received will be added to your total, with those used or sold deducted, ensuring you have a running total of stock at all times. A computerised system will add and deduct these items automatically.

One advantage of completing an annual stocktake is that it will highlight slow-moving items; a stocktaking sale may remove these objects off your shelves whilst making the stocktake easier as it will reduce your gross profit margins. A simple calculation to assess the value of your stock is:

Items of stock at start = 4,000, plus number purchased 8,000 = 12,000 less items used or sold 11,000 = closing stock 1,000 items.

Say the cost of these items is £10 each, but because 200 are damaged their value is reduced to £7.50 each, the closing value of stock is:

800 units @ £10 each = £8,000

200 units @ £7.50 each = £1,500

The gross value of your stock would be £9,500.

It is this last figure that is transferred to your Trading Account. As all items of stock are rotated, stock purchased first is sold before more recently bought items. The cost price of your calculation is taken from the latest invoice received from the supplier.

Trading and Manufacturing Accounts

Before attempting the Profit and Loss Account, there is one other small account to draw up. In a trading firm, one that buys and sells finished products, this account is called the Trading Account and in a manufacturing concern, it is called the Manufacturing Account. The same account in a professional firm is referred to as the Revenue Account.

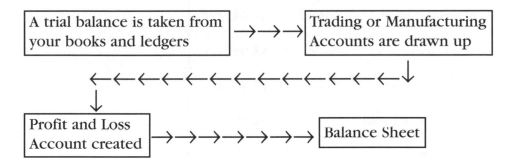

Your path from trial Balance-to-balance Sheet is like the illustration above.

Whatever it is called, the aim of this account is to establish the gross profit of a going concern, and in truth they really all are revenue accounts.

Taking these one at a time, we shall begin with the Trading Account. This account defines the turnover of the business and its gross profit or loss; this final figure is then transferred to the Profit and Loss Account. It is in the Profit and Loss Account that the net profit or loss will be calculated. An average Trading Account will show the following entries:

Trading Account

For the year ending 31 December 2002

	£	£		£
Opening stock		15,500.00	Sales	95,000.00
Purchases	39,000.00		Less returns	3,500.00
Less returns	1,450.00		Net turnover	91,500.00
Net purchases		37,550.00		
Total stock		53,050.00		
Less closing stock		10,460.00		
Cost of stock sold		42,590.00		
Gross profit				
Transferred to P & L a/c		48,910.00		
		91,500.00		91,500.00

Of course, the purchase and sales returns accounts will be closed off and the totals transferred to the Trading Account.

The Manufacturing Accounts will be comparable to those pictured above, but with one main difference. Manufacturers do not buy in goods for resale; they purchase raw materials to make them into finished goods. Therefore, the stock of a manufacturer falls into three categories:

- Stock of raw materials

- Work in progress or partly finished products

- Stock of finished goods

Like all closing stocks, these three items will appear in the Balance Sheet as assets of the business. The Manufacturing Account will be in two parts: the first will be the same as a Trading Account but with the stock classified differently, and below this will be a cost of manufactured goods section; this will include items such as general overheads. These general expenses will include items such as power, rent, rates and wages among others.

Profit and Loss Accounts

When closing off the balances at the time of the trial balance, any losses due to non-payment will be debit balances and these are now transferred to a Bad Debt Account. A Bad Debt Account will list every debt that is considered or proven to be unrecoverable during the course of the year under review.

Any losses during your trading year due to damaged or stolen stock will be reflected in the gross profit figure arrived at in the Trading Account.

Bad Debt Account

Mar 8	Mark Cash	150.00	Dec 31	Transfer to Profit	
Nov 21	P. Sterling	450.00		& Loss a/c.	600.00
		600.00			600.00

In fact, a Profit and Loss Account is no more than a continuation of your Trading Account. Many firms do, in fact, put these two together and produce a Trading and Profit & Loss Account. To arrive at a net profit, the expenses will be listed in your Profit and Loss Account. See the illustration below.

Profit and Loss Account

For the year ending 31 December 2002

	£		£
Bad debts	600.00	Gross profit (transferred from trading a/c.)	48,910.00
Rent & rates	3,350.00		
Wages	9,800.00		
Commission paid	2,100.00		
Printing	250.00		
Total expenses	16,100.00		
Net profit	32,810.00		
	48,910.00		48,910.00

The net profit sum shown in this illustration will now be transferred to the Capital Account. A point to note in respect of your final accounts is that any figure or total that represents a loss is placed within brackets, thus allowing it to be easily recognisable. At this stage of accounting, the double entry system concludes. All that remains now is for the Balance Sheet to be prepared, and any necessary adjustments to the final accounts to be made.

In this guide there has been a lot of accounts omitted, simply because this is not a book targeted to students where an incredible amount of detailed explanation is required, but to the businessperson. After the next sections, the subsequent chapters embrace wages, computerisation and most of all what you can learn from your accounts, and the uses to which they can be put. This in my mind is far more important for today's entrepreneur than learning about the entries your book-keeper will be doing on your behalf anyway. However, it is necessary to provide a basic understanding of what is required to enable the remaining chapters to make sense.

Adjustments to the accounts

The purpose of adjusting the final accounts is to generate an accurate set of accounts and Balance Sheet for the period under examination. One of the main reasons for making an adjustment is payment made or received in advance. Payments nearly always made in advance include insurance premiums, rent and rates. Taking 31 December as your year-end, if you paid three months' rent on the first of December, only one month of that rent would apply to the current year's accounts. So a rental charge of say £3,000 per quarter means the accounts would need to be adjusted to show only £1,000 applicable to the current year with the rest held over to the next accounting period. In this instance, if you took a look at your rent account it will appear as below.

Rent Account

1 Dec	Rent paid	3,000.00	31 Dec	Profit & loss a/c.	1,000.00
			Balance c/d		2,000.00
		3,000.00			3,000.00
1 Jan	Balance b/d	2,000.00			

Payments made in advance to your firm for services not yet rendered cannot be treated as profits, but they will be carried forward to the next trading year as liabilities. The reasoning behind this is that if you are unable for any reason to fulfil your obligations, the money will be returned to your customer.

Another example of an adjustment to your final accounts may be accrued expenses. This usually applies to wages, or commissions due to salespeople. If wages are paid weekly or fortnightly, they may span a year-end. The Wages Account will have entries similar to the above Rent Account, but reversed. The portion of the wages due but not yet paid will therefore show as a current liability in the Balance Sheet.

There are many other adjustments that may be made to the final accounts of a business; provision for bad debts is one, depreciation of assets is another and so is goodwill. Let's take these one at a time. In providing for possible bad debts, if it is usual in your trade for, say, five per cent of debts to be not collectable, the

note
In a small business, it is not really necessary to make adjustments for small items such as telephone bills. The Inland Revenue realises the problems this can cause.

sum of £435.50 will be deducted from the debtor's total under current assets in the Balance Sheet. Simply because a debt is being transferred to a Bad Debt Account, it doesn't mean you have to give up on it. The debt must be pursued until all avenues of collection have been exhausted.

Most other assets of a business such as machinery (but not for bricks and mortar) wear out over a given period. Depreciation reduces the value of the asset over its normal life span. Therefore it can be said that depreciation reduces the profits available for use by the owner. However, it does leave an undistributed wealth in the firm. A prudent manager will invest these funds outside the business to replace the asset when the time comes. Otherwise, the undistributed funds can be frittered away, and the business will have to resort to borrowing to replace worn out machinery.

In respect of leases, should the one you purchase have five years to run, simply deduct a fifth from its purchase price each year.

'Goodwill' is the valuation placed on a going concern over and above the value of its assets. It is a sum that is paid by a buyer of a business to the vendor in expectation of the profits to be made that are directly from the hard work of the previous owner. Goodwill is an intangible asset, and it relates to the relationship the former owner built up with the clientele. The customers of the vendor will continue to use the business because of its reputation of fair dealing. As it is not an asset that can be touched, a new owner will probably write this asset off over a period of between three to five years.

note Assets of a limited company must be shown in the Balance Sheet at the original cost, less depreciation to date, and quoted at its net value. This is required to assist shareholders.

Valuing the goodwill of a business is very difficult indeed; its value is only what a third party is prepared to pay for the customer loyalty that has been built up over the years, through the vendor's hard and honest work.

Accounts of limited companies

The accounts of limited companies differ from sole traders' in a number of ways: first there is the distribution of capital. Investors who become shareholders 'subscribe' the capital of the business, which is then used to purchase assets for the company's use and to generally allow it to run its day-to-day business activities. The number of shareholders in an ordinary company can be as few as two, but in a public company the number can run into thousands.

The most common shares offered by a limited company are 'ordinary' and 'preference' shares. The ordinary shareholders take the greatest risk; as their name implies, preference shareholders have preferential treatment when it comes to the payment of dividends - they are always paid first if the company gets into difficulties. Whilst an ordinary shareholder may lose their money if the company fails, they do enjoy a larger share of the profits when times are good.

Loans to a company from sources other than shareholders are called 'debenture'. A debenture is a loan secured upon the company's assets. There are two types of debenture: fixed and floating. Fixed debentures are secured on the firm's fixed assets,

note

Dividends are never guaranteed, except to preference shareholders. Dividend payments are paid at the discretion of the directors of a company.

and if interest is not paid at regular intervals, the assets can be seized and sold to recoup the money loaned. Floating debentures are secured on circulating assets, such as stock.

The accounts and Balance Sheet pertaining to a limited company vary from those of a sole trader inasmuch as not all the profits will be paid to the owners; the company may retain some for future use. The proportion of profit that is retained is transferred to an 'Appropriation Account'. A Balance Sheet is required by statute to set out the assets of a limited company in a certain order. First, the fixed assets are split into three:

- Intangible assets - goodwill and other legal rights.

- Tangible assets - such as premises, etc.

- Trade investments - these are investments in subsidiary companies.

Current assets are also displayed in strict order of:

- Stock

- Debtors

- Other investments

One can bring the current liabilities over to the assets side and show them as a deduction from the current assets. This presents you with the net working capital of your business, and when added to the fixed assets provide you with the net value of assets. There are one or two other items where the accounts of a limited

> **TIP** Don't ever be put off by the Balance Sheet - it's only a snapshot of what your business owes you at a particular moment in time.

company differ from that of a sole trader, but as they are purely of a cosmetic nature, they have little effect on the running of a business and are best left alone.

Year on year consistency in accounts

The idea behind the production of final accounts is to provide you and your shareholders with a financial picture of your business at the end of each year of trading. To enable you to measure any decline or progress of your business from year to year, the annual accounts must be prepared in a uniform manner; otherwise it will be impossible to use them as a gauge.

Accountants will prepare your final accounts on the basis that your business is a 'going concern', i.e. that the business will continue to trade in the foreseeable future. On the other hand, if they have reason to believe the business will cease to trade in the near future, they have a

> **note** The principles of accounting are many, but the two mentioned in this chapter are the most commonly used in today's environment.

duty to amend the value of the firm's assets. To illustrate this point, say the machinery used in your business is valued at £5,000 as a 'going concern'; this machinery will be making you money and any buyers of your business will gladly pay this price, because the value it provides will be passed onto them. Now, if your business ceases to trade, the machinery will not be earning its keep, and if it is something that has very limited use it can only be sold as scrap, meaning it has little or no value. So in the preparation of your final accounts, you have an obligation to inform your accountant if there is any likelihood the business will close.

Another prudent principle of accounting is that businesspeople and their accountants do not take profit into account until it is actually realised, but they do take account of losses as soon as they occur. At the first hint that a loss is possible, the offending account is transferred to a Suspense Account, thus making provision for a bad debt.

note

Manufacturing, trading, and Profit and Loss Accounts must take into account all income received, plus what is due and yet to be received.

However, it should be noted that whilst this principle works in the case of, for example, stock, the opposite applies to property. If you purchase 100 items of stock at £1 each, and demand is such that their current value is £2 and 50 items remain in stock, you cannot say you have made £50 profit on that stock until you sell them. This is due to the fact that between valuing your stock and selling it, the demand may plummet, and those items are now worth considerably less, leaving you with a loss situation. How the prudent businessperson handles this situation will be seen when reading the section relating to Profit and Loss Accounts.

With regard to property, increases in property value tend to remain stable; only on rare occasions do property prices nose-dive. By taking this appreciation into account, one wards off predators thinking of taking over your business simply to sell its premises and thereby taking the profit for themselves. This practice, known as asset stripping, was rife in the 1960s.

Budgets & cash flow forecasts

Chapter 6

Budgets & cash flow forecasts

What you'll find in this chapter:

⫸ Budgeting and cash flow forecasting

⫸ Costing and pricing

⫸ Computerised accounting

Most of the principles of book-keeping covered so far have related to transactions that have already taken place. Whilst this historical record is essential in measuring the success of your business, it is just as important to plan for the future.

Get into the habit of producing and reviewing your budget and cash flow forecasts on a regular basis and your efforts will be well rewarded, for it will be sound budgeting that will get your business through those times when a sudden unforeseen downturn in sales occurs.

Budgets and cash flow forecasting

Smoothing out the flow of cash is far more difficult in some businesses than in others. There are some firms whose cash flow rarely varies from one month to another, while others get seasonal peaks. Toy manufacturers, for example, make

their products throughout the year, but mostly sell them at Christmas, leaving them with only January and February to collect their mainstream income.

It is no use assuming that your customers will pay you in 45 days, when historically they take 60 to settle their accounts. When you start up or purchase a business, a cash flow forecast is required for periods of anything of up to two or three years. If you are borrowing money, the longer the period of review, the better. With an ongoing business, a three-monthly forecast is usual, although six-monthly intervals are preferred.

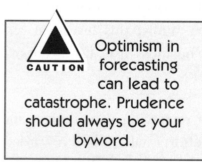

CAUTION Optimism in forecasting can lead to catastrophe. Prudence should always be your byword.

Budgeting for cash flow is, in simple terms, only a prediction of the likely income and expenditure you will need in order to manage your business efficiently during the period under review. The usual way to do this is to draw up an analysis page or spreadsheet and divide it up as per the sample below.

In this example, you will notice that in January, against forecast, there is an actual shortfall of £500, which could easily be made up from your own

Cash Flow	January		February		March	
	Budget £	Actual £	Budget £	Actual £	Budget £	Actual £
Sales (cash)	4,000	3,350	4,500		6,000	
Debts collected	6,500	6,150	6,500		7,500	
Other receipts	500	500	500		500	
Total receipts	11,000	10,000	11,500		14,000	
Stock payments	5,000	5,200	5,500		5,500	
Wages	5,250	5,300	4,500		4,500	
Insurance			1,500			
Rent			2,000			
Total outgoings	10,250	10,500	13,500		10,000	

resources. But add that to the additional outgoings forecast for February and it becomes obvious that you will need to arrange overdraft facilities to compensate you until the profit forecast in March.

The actual columns obviously cannot be completed until after the relevant month-ends, at which point the appropriate figures will be inserted and then analysed. If, as in the above example, an overdraft is required, this will be brought into that particular month's budget; it will then have to be added to the costs of borrowing in the outgoing section.

When you know the pattern of your cash flow you can do a little smoothing out. For example, if you spot a period ahead when there is going to be more cash available than you need to operate successfully, it may be prudent to plan the replacement of, say, worn out machinery at that time. On the other hand, if a shortfall appears to be imminent, it may be possible to arrange for early payment of some accounts by offering a discount.

The comparison of budgeted and actual figures is called 'variance analysis'. If the actual figures vary from your budget investigation and show that the difference is due to a rise of stock prices, the higher cost must be passed on to your customers. If the variance is due to the wastage of resources, you must deal with the problem immediately to eradicate the waste.

> **TIP** When forecasting your cash flow, remember that cash sales will be shown in the month they occur, but payments for credit sales may not be received until the next month or even later.

Costing and pricing

One of the trickiest problems in business is striking the right balance between costing and pricing. If you charge too much, customers will stay away in droves; but price your goods too cheaply and your firm could be heading towards ruin.

> **note** Trying to compete on low prices alone is never a sound strategy, but add in customer service to a fair price policy and you have the key to success.

One aspect many small business owners forget to take into account when it comes to costs is their own time. The cost of an owner's time is usually the dearest in a firm. Staff outlay, and this especially applies to consulting firms, is the most important component of your costs; so always ensure time spent working for clients is properly recorded.

The best method to use when pricing your goods is to start with how much stock you think you will sell in a week.

Let's say you sell on average £5,000 worth of stock weekly. If your average overhead costs amount to £600, and your time comes to £400, this means you must sell your goods for at least £6,000 to break even. Therefore, in order to obtain a net profit, the price of your goods must be marked up. A 30 per cent mark up on the above figures will provide you with a net profit of £1,800.

After deciding upon a fair price, one that attracts customers whilst at the same time providing you with a good living, it would be wrong to think your price is now set in stone. Say a large firm moves into your area and they approach you to purchase supplies of tea and coffee, plus a few varied snack items for their workers.

note Learning how to price your goods competitively, and still remain in profit, requires the agility to walk a tightrope whilst balancing the needs of your customers and family.

They anticipate spending on average £520 per week and to save them going along to the wholesalers and opening an account, they suggest you offer them a 15 per cent discount. From these extra sales you will be earning another £60 per week profit and your overheads will remain unchanged. Now doesn't it make good business sense to be flexible about your pricing policy?

From time to time, pricing becomes an art form rather than a strict business strategy; at these times the above standards should assist you in taking the guesswork out of any modifications you might be forced to make.

Computerised accounting

It is advisable for even the smallest business to computerise its book-keeping system. The cost of a suitable computer and the appropriate software is such that the price alone shouldn't be a barrier, and the cost is more than compensated by the hours it will save you. Computerising your accounts should be given priority in a small business, in preference to employing a book-keeper. Another cost saver will be the accountant's fees at the year-end because a lot of their work will already be summarised for them.

Most computers come with a spreadsheet program which you can use for your accounts. By drawing up a table with the headings mentioned earlier and using this as a template, you will be able to work on them, and save and reload them under a separate heading whenever you like.

Using computers in book-keeping changes the records you will need. Instead of copying documents into a daybook and transferring the details to a ledger, the one entry you key in will make all the entries you require simultaneously.

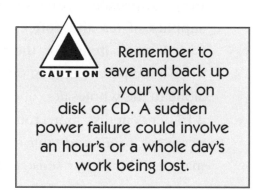

CAUTION Remember to save and back up your work on disk or CD. A sudden power failure could involve an hour's or a whole day's work being lost.

So when you want an invoice or credit note prepared, the computer software will do the book-keeping entries at the same time. When a sale invoice is created, for example, the sales, debtors and VAT accounts will be completed at the same time. On the other hand, if you require a summary of your firm's income and expenses, the computer will compile a report at a click of a mouse, or touch of a button for you to review.

As your system will be updated as you go along, it is possible to produce a Profit and Loss Account on a daily basis. Apart from keeping a record of all your business transactions, your computer will list all your business contacts. Another important benefit of being computerised is the instant production of personalised sales literature or letters chasing up late paying customers.

Inputting data couldn't be simpler; the instructions that come up on your screen require you to complete a number of straightforward little boxes. In addition, when paying your suppliers you can even have remittance advices and cheques printed.

Retailers should bear in mind that they will need an electronic point of sale (EPOS) add-on if they wish to use bar coding in their business or accept credit or debit card payments.

TIP Always keep in mind it's not the computers that make mistakes; it's the humans that operate them.

There are many software packages currently on the market, ranging from about £150 to a few thousand pounds. Check them out carefully to ensure you get the right package for your business.

Payroll

Chapter 7

Payroll

What you'll find in this chapter:

⇒ Payroll calculations and book-keeping

⇒ Tax credits and other items

It doesn't matter if you are employing someone for the first time or you have dozens of employees on your payroll; using other people in your business brings with it certain responsibilities. There is the requirement to keep a record of salaries and wages paid, the deduction of tax and national insurance contributions, and in recent years the amount of legislation has grown enormously.

Distinguishing between taking on an employee or someone who is self-employed is essential, as it affects the way you account for the payment made to them. Whilst employing someone on a self-employed basis removes the need to deduct tax and other contributions, and is generally more convenient for you, do not try to pass off a genuine employee as one who is self-

---

employed. Although the Inland Revenue will supply you with guidelines, here are a few points to consider in identifying who is an employee:

- Will the person working for you also be working for other people? The more they work for other people the more they could be considered self-employed.

- If they are free to leave once their task is completed, or at any other time at their discretion, then this is a sign of self-employment.

- Do they get paid holidays, and sick leave, or use of a company car? Then they are probably employees.

- Can they send someone else to do their work? If so, they are self-employed.

The above list is not exhaustive. Those factors listed will be considered along with a number of other working practices by the Inland Revenue to determine the true picture.

A visit to your local tax office will provide you with all the information needed, as will a visit to the Inland Revenue website. Among the featured areas on the site are:

Informing the Inland Revenue you have taken on an employee will bring you a detailed set of instructions explaining how to calculate the required deductions, by return.

- Starting up a business

- Tax credits

- Guidelines for employees using their cars for work

- E-business and e-commerce

- Guides for consultants (IR35)

- Construction industry schemes

Various leaflets can also be ordered at www.inlandrevenue.gov.uk.

Payroll calculations and book-keeping

We may as well look at the calculations for payroll at the same time as the book-keeping. In practice, you will use either a payroll bureau or a computer package to do the calculations.

Taking the case of a single employee earning a monthly salary of £1,000, in the absence of any other considerations, the basic accounting entries will be:

| DEBIT | Payroll expense | £1,000 |
| CREDIT | Payroll control | £1,000 |

Remember, we <u>debit</u> expense because it is one of the costs which are deducted from sales to calculate the profit which belongs to the owners of the business, who are <u>creditors</u>.

The credit on the payroll control account will be cleared when the employee is paid, but, as we all know, an employee does not receive all of his salary. The employer deducts Income Tax and National Insurance and pays it to the Government (by the 19th of the following month) on behalf of the employee. The deductions are calculated using books of tables issued by the Inland Revenue, a complicated procedure which a bureau or computer can perform easily. The accounting entries will look like this:

DEBIT	Payroll expense	£1,000
CREDIT	Payroll control	£700
CREDIT	Inland Revenue	£300

Finally, we have to deal with the employer's National Insurance contribution. This is an extra cost borne by the employer, on top of the salary paid to the employee. Supposing the employer's NI in this case is £159, the book-keeping entries will be:

| DEBIT | Payroll expense | £150 |
| CREDIT | Payroll control | £150 |

The account will now look as follows:

Payroll expense

Salary	1,000	
Employer's NI	150	
	1,150	

Inland Revenue control

	Employer's NI	1,000
	Employee's NI & PAYE	150
		1,150

Payroll control

	Net salary	700
		700

The payroll acount is debited and cleared when the employee receives his net pay. The Inland Revenue control account is cleared when the tax and National Insurance are paid to the Inland Revenue.

Tax credits and other items

Other elements of pay to take into consideration are Statutory Sick Pay, maternity leave and pay, and tax credits. Tax credits are incorporated into the employee's tax code and are added to their pay; the sum paid will be reclaimed by the employer in due course from the tax collected from the remaining workers when accounting to the Inland Revenue. This method of payment is extremely convenient for the Government as a large number of payments can be made without any administrative expenses. Since the businessperson is deducting tax each week to hand over to the Inland Revenue, it is easy to deduct these payments from the tax due.

At present there are three separate tax credits businesspeople must currently handle; in the future, there may be more:

Working family tax credits is a scheme designed to give low-paid working families a better deal financially. It is paid via the employee's pay packet.

> **note** All those who are self-employed are required to use the self-assessment system. While this removes the need for proper accounts, nonetheless keeping proper accounts does allow for better financial control.

Disabled person's tax credit was created to assist people with illness or disability to return to, or take up, paid employment by topping up their earnings. It is also available to self-employed disabled people. Again it is paid through their salaries, except for the self-employed, who get it paid directly to them.

Children's tax credit is provided to help people with a child or children under the age of 16 years living with them, by reducing the amount of income tax they need to pay. It is operated through the tax coding system.

Putting accounting data to work

Chapter 8

Putting accounting data to work

What you'll find in this chapter:

⇒ Monthly financial reports

⇒ Statistical control figures and their uses

⇒ Efficiency ratios

⇒ Liquidity ratios

⇒ Profitability ratios

⇒ Purchasing a business

⇒ Ledger entries for merging and buying a business

Many small business owners spend hours toiling over their bookkeeping duties, recording every transaction and ensuring the accounts balance. Keeping control of your debtors and creditors makes sense, but accounts can be used for much more than that.

Your books are bursting with information you can be putting to good use. It is surprising how many businesspeople think that once the invoices, delivery notes and cash transactions are recorded and filed, the books can be put in a drawer and forgotten about until next time.

Ratios, which are dealt with later, can be a gauge to the strengths and weaknesses of your business. They will also help you to assess the viability of any business you may wish to purchase. Knowing if your business is contracting or expanding will help you make the right management decisions. Other information that may

> **note** Knowing how to interpret your Profit and Loss Account, Balance Sheet and other accounting data is the key to financial and business success.

come to light when interpreting your accounts is if one item of stock is selling slower or faster than other lines. It will also tell you if stock or cash is being misappropriated. All these and a multitude of other data are sitting in your accounts just waiting to be used.

Monthly financial reports

These are sometimes referred to as management accounts, and can be used by owner/managers, departmental heads or directors. The kind of information they have to offer varies from budgeting, cash flow forecasting, pricing and costing, and variance analysis, to more detailed reporting from the purchase and sales ledgers.

> **TIP** Businesses who pay their suppliers on time not only get better deals, but their reputations are enhanced and this can translate into more sales.

Purchase ledger reports cover three areas - one is the analysis of expenses. Using the analysis pages referred to in earlier chapters with your previously prepared budget, you can tell if resources are being used efficiently. The other area of importance to you should be stock management, and this includes work in progress for manufacturing businesses. You have to achieve a balance between having money tied up in excessively high stock levels and risking lost sales by being out of stock.

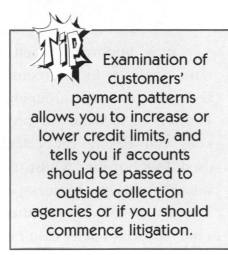

Examination of customers' payment patterns allows you to increase or lower credit limits, and tells you if accounts should be passed to outside collection agencies or if you should commence litigation.

Another useful report is the 'aged creditors' report'. This lists all the people to whom you owe money, detailing the amounts due to each and the age of the liability.

Sales ledger reports, on the other hand, will help you to keep control of your debtors. An aged sales ledger report will list your debtors and the size and age of their outstanding balances. Measuring collection performance is an essential part of cash flow management.

These reports and calculations are available to you instantly using a computerised system of book-keeping. They naturally take a little longer to prepare with a manual system, but the information provided is essential for the profitable operation of your business.

Statistical control figures and their uses

Credit managers use ratio analysis in assessing risk management in banking and the financial health of a customer in trade. Entrepreneurs use it to confirm the viability of a company when buying a business; the business owner should be using it to measure current performance against historical achievement. In other words, it helps you to understand how your business is developing. By using three or more years' trading figures, you have a useful gauge of how your business is doing.

note Ratios are a means of comparing one figure with another to generate a connection between them, and to link different parts of your accounts.

It is important when using ratio analysis to be consistent; always use the same grouping, such as assets to liabilities, or profits to sales and ensure the calculation used does not vary. Whilst they are valuable tools in a businessperson's armoury, misuse or abuse them and they may become insignificant. A profit to the balance of petty cash ratio, for example, would be absolutely of no use to you, but total borrowings to net worth ratio will be very helpful.

Ratios can also be used to compare the results of your business with others in the same industry sector.

Efficiency ratios

These concentrate on the efficient use of funds in your organisation. To see how well you are controlling your finances, they look at the working capital part of your accounts, such as stock, debtors and creditors.

There are three ways you can handle stock to sales ratios; the idea is to use the one best for your business and stick to it. At all times, the method of calculation must be consistent.

1. $\dfrac{\text{Stock} \times 365}{\text{Sales}}$ = Number of days stock is held

2. $\dfrac{\text{Stock}}{\text{Sales}}$ = Stock turnover ratio

3. $\dfrac{\text{Sales}}{\text{Stock}}$ = Number of times stock is turned over

Out of the above samples, the first ratio relating to the number of days a stock is held before being sold is the most noteworthy. You should bear in mind that this ratio can vary greatly in different types of businesses. A florist, for example, may only hold stock for a day or so, whilst the time a furniture retailer holds stock can run into months.

The important feature with any ratio is the trend it picks up. An increase in the number of day's stock you are holding may be an indication you are holding obsolete stock, or unsaleable, damaged items. In the fashion trade, it can mean you or your buyer are not as chic as you think you are.

Other ratios in respect of purchase and sales ledgers are:

$\dfrac{\text{Debtors} \times 365}{\text{Sales}}$ = the time it takes you to collect payment from your customers

In an ideal world, the number of days should liken closely to your terms of trade. The faster you collect the money owing to your business the better. A trend showing the number of days increasing could mean you have no control over your debtors, and this will require an investigation.

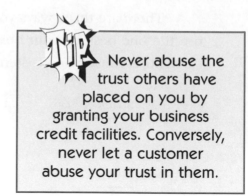

TIP Never abuse the trust others have placed on you by granting your business credit facilities. Conversely, never let a customer abuse your trust in them.

Again the opposite applies in your purchase ledger ratios but the same calculation applies:

$$\frac{\text{Creditors x } 365}{\text{Purchases}} = \text{the time in days it takes you to pay suppliers}$$

Whilst any lengthening of this trend will improve your cash flow, this can only prove to be a short-term advantage. If suppliers start to remove credit facilities from you, this will have a severe impact upon your trading.

Liquidity ratios

These examine the affiliation between assets and liabilities. They are used to ensure that you have a sufficient cycle of funds running through your business to pay creditors. That means stocks and debtors are being turned into cash to provide you with ample cash flow.

Whilst the ratio of current assets divided by current liabilities requires a ratio of two to denote a healthy business, this will mean you have twice as many assets to meet your liabilities as they fall due, but this assumes your stock is readily convertible into cash. As this may be impossible in reality, a liquidity ratio excluding stock would be a far better gauge to use. This is computed in the following manner:

$$\frac{\text{Cash} + \text{Debtors}}{\text{Current Liabilities}}$$

If the resulting answer is less than one, then you have a liquidity problem and you may be unable to meet your debts as they become payable. This is a sign that your profits are being eroded, or that you are now currently in a loss-making situation.

One of the most applied ratios banks and finance houses use, especially invoice factors, is the debt to equity ratio, or 'gearing ratio'. This determines the amount of funds in a business and the amounts borrowed from outside the firm. This ratio uses the following formula, and the resulting number should therefore be greater than one:

$$\frac{\text{Total borrowing}}{\text{Net worth}}$$

Lenders will also take into account the quality of the proposition before them. Consequently, it is an essential asset to any business to have a strong business plan presented by a business owner who readily understands the financial position of his firm and is able to talk finance.

note Each lender has different lending guidelines, but generally speaking the amount being borrowed should not exceed the net worth of your business.

Profitability ratios

Naturally, this ratio examines the trend in the profit margins of your business. Previously in this book, gross and net profits were shown in the Balance Sheet and Profit and Loss Accounts. The method used to determine these ratios is the same for gross and net profits; the only difference being that in the demonstrated calculation either the word 'net' or 'gross' should be inserted before the word 'profit'.

$$\frac{Profits \times 100}{Sales}$$

There will be variations of this ratio depending on the type of business you are running. A retailer who has a high sales volume but a low mark-up on his or her stock will differ from that of a manufacturer who has high overhead costs. A trend showing a decline in the gross profit ratio needs to be looked into very quickly for it could mean the following:

- Your pricing strategy is wrong.

- Increased purchasing costs are not being passed onto your customers.

- Margins are being eroded due to competition.

Whatever the reason for a reducing gross profit ratio, urgent action will need to be taken.

On the other hand, a net profit ratio reflects on the funds being retained in the business to finance expansion. This ratio can be affected by variations in your gross profits; a declining movement not matched by a similar move in gross profits could indicate your expenses are getting out of hand. A review of any increased expenditure will enable cost savings to be implemented.

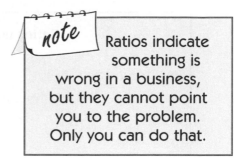

note Ratios indicate something is wrong in a business, but they cannot point you to the problem. Only you can do that.

In looking at the above ratios, it is assumed the resultant figures show a negative position. However, there are times when ratios improve; this could be for a number of reasons. Training makes the staff more efficient; a member of staff leaves who is generous with your stock; or the staff take more care and breakages become less frequent. Perhaps improved buying methods, or increased sales can be adding to an improvement in profits. When this happens and it is down to an employee, reward them. That's why bonuses were invented, to provide incentives for efficiency over and above the normal line of duty.

Other useful ratios

The number of ratios mentioned so far represents only a few of the ratios available for use by the enterprising businessperson. The number used in your own business will depend upon the individual owner; certainly anyone purchasing a business will need to investigate the proposed acquisition in depth, possibly using the full list of ratios that can be found below, to ensure that they have the fullest financial picture.

Ratios used in the interpretation of accounts

Profit/net assets: Indicates the degree of success in utilising assets to generate profits. The profit figure should include both operating and other income, but after depreciation charges and before interest and tax.

Sales growth: Current year's sales as a percentage of prior years less than 100 per cent means a decline in sales.

Profit growth: Current year's profits as a percentage of prior years, to be compared with sales growth. A less proportionate growth in profit compared to sales is a matter of concern.

Sales/net assets: Indicates success in use of assets to create sales; an improving ratio between one year and the next is favourable.

Sales/fixed assets: Indicates efficient use of premises, plant and equipment. A high ratio suggests a labour-intensive rather than capital-intensive business. Will explain a profit/sales ratio that is lower than industry norm.

Sales/net current assets: Measures the successful use of working capital. An excessively high ratio is a sign of overtrading.

Sales/net worth: Another indicator in detecting overtrading. It is important to remove intangible assets, e.g. goodwill from the calculations.

Fixed assets/total assets: This ratio will be higher in a non-manufacturing business. Compare with profit growth to evaluate if fixed assets are being used productively.

Purchasing a business

Entrepreneurs investigating a business they intend purchasing are reminded of the importance the above indicators can play in their decision-making process. Placed alongside information obtained from other sources such as Dunn & Bradstreet Ltd and Extel Financial Ltd, they will be invaluable in assessing your new business venture.

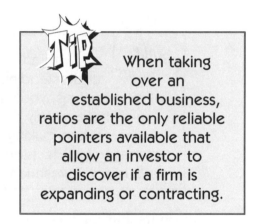

Once they see for themselves how the business has performed over previous years, they can then weigh up what the prognosis is for its future. Not only will your deliberations bring you to an appropriate purchase price, it will also provide you with an insight into the action you may need to take on completing the acquisition.

When taking over an established business, ratios are the only reliable pointers available that allow an investor to discover if a firm is expanding or contracting.

A business that is in decline should not necessarily be pushed aside. Business turn-around situations excite the serial entrepreneur, so they will not automatically be put off. With the right management expertise, many unprofitable businesses make money for new owners. Sometimes these businesses change hands for as little as a nominal price of £1. But this usually means a lot of debt is being transferred to the new owners.

As you can see, there is a whole lot of information buried in a set of accounts that can be very helpful to a purchaser of a business, as well as its owner.

When it comes to buying a going concern, one thing always to keep in mind is that the value a vendor puts on his or her business sometimes bears no relation to its true value. The best approach for a buyer is to assume the business is valueless and then attempt to qualify every pound that you offer against the profit potential of the business.

Always price insolvent firms by valuing their assets on a forced sale basis.

note With an understanding of ratio analysis, you will never have to rely on others when making management decisions or business investments.

Much of the information written about buying a business in this book has revolved around a profitable trading or manufacturing concern. Valuing a service business can be very tricky indeed. There are usually very few tangible assets, and all the vendor has to sell is their existing customer accounts and mailing list. Sales can be tied to the goodwill of the existing vendor; once the business transfers to the new owner, these customers may disappear overnight. Extreme caution is required, and any price agreed upon should be based on achievable future profits and not on historical records.

Ledger entries for merging and buying a business

To record the purchase of a business acquired from a sole trader requires you, as the buyer, to agree a price acceptable to you and the vendor. Assuming a purchase price of £125,000 has been agreed between yourself and Mr. Ted Knavish for his garage, your first task is to record the value of the items included in the contract that you have received. The list of assets you would put together must be based on your valuations, and not those of the vendor. A typical list of assets you should draw up needs to resemble the example provided below. You will note in the model shown that the total amount of assets is valued at less than the price that you paid. This difference represents the value you place upon the goodwill of the business. When the opening entries are made, the goodwill figure of £10,000.00 must be entered into your accounts.

In addition to the accounts mentioned in Chapter 4, a purchase of business account will be required together with a goodwill account. Opening balances for these accounts will be taken from your list of assets, shown below:

Assets included in the purchase of garage from T Knavish.

	£
Premises	60,000.00
Fixtures & fittings	10,000.00
Motor vehicles	35,000.00
Stock	15,000.00
	120,000.00
Less the liabilities of trade creditors	5,000.00
	115,000.00

When two sole traders merge, an agreement is reached prior to the merger on whose assets will be sold and whose will be retained. So it is possible that one of the new partners will bring more cash into the business, while the other will be donating more assets; but the overall value of the new business partnership will normally be equally shared. The general day-to-day book-keeping requirements of the newly merged business will be no different to the partnership accounts discussed in the next chapter.

note When buying a profitable business, the purchase price usually includes a sum for goodwill over and above the value of the assets being transferred.

However, both owners of the new business must each draw up a statement of affairs. This statement is no more than a list of assets every partner is bringing to the newly merged firm. The entries from the statement of affairs will now be transferred into a combined Balance Sheet.

The transfer of ownership of a limited company, on the other hand, can be said to be a little simpler. The actual transfer takes place with the purchase of the company's shares. Apart from recording the change of share ownership in the share register, no other book-keeping entries are required. The assets including stock, creditors, debtors and everything else owned by the company still belong to the company; nothing else has altered except a few share certificates being handed from one person to another in exchange for cash.

Partnership accounts & tax cutting tips

9

Chapter 9

Partnership accounts & tax cutting tips

What you'll find in this chapter:

➠ Partnership accounts

➠ Source and application of funds

➠ Tips for cutting tax and avoiding an Inland Revenue probe

By now you should have a reasonable working knowledge of how book-keeping works in your business. The information you can now obtain from your books will ensure your business is going in the right direction. However, there are one or two other items I feel may benefit you, if not now, then at some time in the future.

Partnership accounts

Although the book-keeping system of a partnership varies little from that of a sole trader, there are certain aspects in the final accounts that do differ. Whilst we tend to see fewer partnerships in general trading concerns, partnerships do still exist in the professions.

> **note** The Partnership Act 1890 is there to settle disputes between partners, but rulings under this Act are avoidable by partners agreeing between themselves and drawing up an agreement in writing.

A major problem with partnerships, like marriage, is that whilst everything can be sweetness and light in the beginning, as time goes by people's circumstances alter and disagreements can cause unsolvable problems. A partnership deed, like a prenuptial agreement, will go a long way to avoid arguments occurring later that may have a detrimental effect on the profitable operation of the business.

Unless you are a solicitor, it is not advisable to draw up a partnership deed without legal assistance. The essence of the deed should be the:

- date the partnership begins, and its proposed duration;

- ratio of capital being provided by each partner, and how the profits or losses will be divided;

- amount of drawings each partner is allowed against anticipated profits;

- method by which disputes will be settled;

- arrangements, which are to be made in the event of a partner's death, or a new partner joining.

Unlike a sole trader, the original capital of a partnership does not vary. So instead of profits or losses being added or subtracted along with drawings from a Trading Account, each partner will have the following two accounts opened in his or her name:

- A Capital Account in which will be recorded the amount of original capital invested.

- A Current Account showing day to day payments to and from each partner.

Each year, the Capital Accounts will be shown in the Balance Sheet, listed in order of the amount invested and not alphabetically. The Trading and Profit and Loss Accounts will be no different from those of a sole trader, except that the interest on any loans made by a partner will not be paid out but transferred to their current account.

It should be stated that where partners contribute unequal amounts of capital, interest is paid, thus giving more to those who took greater risks. There is little point in awarding interest payments when capital is invested in equal shares. The Appropriation Account would show the following entries in addition to the interest element if apt:

- Goodwill

- Partnership salaries

- Residue of profits or losses

If no agreement has been drawn up, then any profits or losses will be

> **note**
> Partnership accounts differ chiefly from other accounts when the time comes to allocate profits or losses, then an 'Appropriation Account' is opened.

shared equally between all partners under the terms of the Partnership Act referred to earlier.

An example of the two accounts relating to a partnership over and above those of a sole trader or limited company are displayed below:

Balance Sheet
As at 31 December 2002

		£	£
Capital at start			
P. Sterling		15,000	
K. Turner		15,000	
			30,000

Appropriation Account

		£			£
31 Dec	Goodwill	5,000	31 Dec	Net profit	31,000
	Salary	20,000			
Share of residue profit					
31 Dec P.S.	3,000				
K.T.	3,000	6,000			
		31,000			31,000

Source and application of funds

It is important to realise the difference between financial resources and cash. Just because your business is in profit, it doesn't necessarily mean the profit is held in cash.

In real life, what happens when money is generated from a sale is that it is immediately reinvested into your business, and that also means the profit element. By purchasing more goods that are again turned into cash, more profits are made. However, because this cycle is an ongoing situation, there is no actual cash pile to hoard. This also applies if you had purchased assets with your profits.

Understanding where your funds are coming from and going to are as important as budgeting and cash flow forecasting. This is undoubtedly one management tool that can especially help small businesses. An 'application of funds statement' is an addition to your Profit and Loss and Balance Sheet.

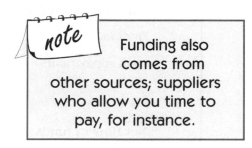

note

Funding also comes from other sources; suppliers who allow you time to pay, for instance.

In coming to terms with funding, it should be remembered that although depreciation is a charge against profits, it is only a book-keeping entry.

An application and source of funds report is produced below. This statement gives an indication of how the report should look. A corresponding Profit and Loss Account and Balance Sheet have not been produced as specimens are provided elsewhere, although the figures shown would have been taken from these two reports.

SOURCE OF FUNDS	£
Profit	35,500.00
Depreciation (added back)	9,000.00
Generated profit	43,500.00
Capital introduced	50,000.00
Loans (Long term)	10,000.00
Government training grant	2,500.00
Total source of funds	106,000.00
APPLICATION OF FUNDS	
Purchase of fixed assets	40,000.00
Drawings	10,000.00
Loan repayments	2,000.00
	52,000.00
Net flow of funds	54,000.00
WORKING CAPITAL	
Stock	21,000.00
Debtors	12,000.00
Cash/bank	22,500.00
Creditors (increase -)	1,500.00
Net increase in funds	54,000.00

When preparing your statement of funds report, either historical or projected figures can be used. Remember to keep to the format of whichever one you have chosen and do not intermingle the two sets of figures.

The basic ingredients of a source and application of funds statement are:

- Adjusted profit or loss for the period under review (the removal of non cash items)

- Amount of dividends paid (if any)

- Acquisitions and disposal of fixed assets

- Increases in share capital or loans

- Any increase or decrease in working capital (current assets)

All these items have been reflected in the above diagram.

This statement should never be used to replace your cash flow forecasts, as it cannot supply you with information relating to your day-to-day working capital requirements; as its title suggests, it can only tell you where the funding will come from.

> **TIP** It is important to retain control of both your debtors and creditors at all times to ensure adequate flow of funds to your business.

Tips for cutting tax and avoiding an Inland Revenue probe

I do not profess to be an expert on taxation but as a businessman of many years' standing I have acquired a little bit of knowledge on the subject. The people working for the Inland Revenue are not fools. Learn this valuable lesson and respect them, and you are on your way to avoiding that dreaded investigation, which I am sure they enjoy springing on unwary businesspeople from time to time.

However, they do have a weakness and that's their uniformity. They work on a basis that if the average builder, for example, earns profits at the rate of 25 per cent, then every builder does. So if they spot a builder claiming a profit margin of only 15 per cent, they tend to get suspicious. Unless you can come up with a reasonable explanation when submitting your returns, they will start asking some awkward questions.

It is now easier for the Inland Revenue to pick firms at random and investigate them; at one time they had to have a valid reason, but not any more. So the answer is to make sure your profits are unified with your business sector norm, and not like our builder above. Offshore trusts or loans to directors that will in time be forgotten about can all bring the wrath of the taxman down upon you like a ton of bricks.

> 'No man is obliged to arrange his affairs in a way that enables the Inland Revenue to take the largest slice of his income' - loosely quoted - Lord Clyde 1927.

What can be done to reduce your tax burden? Make sure you claim all the allowable expenses you can. There are times when you can't get a receipt, so people think they cannot claim, but the Inland Revenue will allow expenses for car parking and postage stamps without a receipt. Another way to claim for expenses that are incurred on a regular basis legally is to arrange a dispensation with them. Other useful tax initiatives are:

- Make allowances in your accounts for bad debts.

- Fund directors' pensions from the company.

- If you are a sole trader, become a limited company; you can split your taxable income with your spouse and by taking your income as dividends you'll avoid paying National Insurance contributions.

Owner/directors should claim for all out-of-pocket expenses they incur from the company, even if they are not allowable tax costs such as entertaining, to avoid paying for these items out of their own taxed income. Here are some examples of other types of costs that you are able to write off against your firm's tax bill:

- IT and internet phones - 100 per cent

- Investment that cuts energy use or greenhouse gases - 100 per cent

- VAT that you have been charged but cannot pass on - 100 per cent

- New cars (to a maximum of £12,000) - 25 per cent per year

Fines and entertainment, including entertainment for export clients are not allowable expenses, and these items cannot reduce the amount of tax you pay.

For a more detailed explanation of what can and cannot be done as far as the Inland Revenue is concerned, a word with your accountant or a specialist tax adviser is strongly recommended.

Glossary of accounting terms

Take a careful look at the following terms used in book-keeping and accountancy work and you'll soon become adept at understanding what your book-keeper or accountant is doing for you. They will make your task a lot easier in making representations to bank managers and other potential lenders, especially if you are clear about their definitions.

Accounts	Financial records, where business transactions are entered and double entry book-keeping takes place.
Assets	Items owned by a business.
Capital	The amount of the owner's stake in a business.
Cash purchases	Goods bought and paid for immediately.
Cash sales	Goods sold, with immediate payment received in cash, cheque, credit card or debit card.
Credit purchases	Goods bought, with payment to be made at a later date.
Credit sales	Goods sold, with payment to be received at an agreed date in the future.
Creditors	Individuals or businesses to whom money is owed by the business.
Debtors	Individuals or businesses who owe money in respect of goods or services supplied by your business.
Double entry	The debiting and crediting of accounts.

Expenses The costs of running the business on a day-to-day basis, e.g. wages, rent, telephone, etc.

Ledger The three sections into which accounts are traditionally divided: sales, purchases and general.

Liabilities Items owed by a business.

Profit The excess of income over expenses made by a business from selling goods overseas during a particular time period.

Purchases Goods bought that are intended for resale.

Sales The sale of goods, whether on credit or for cash, in which the business trades.

Turnover The total of sales, both cash and credit, for a particular time period.

Index

A

accountants 9, 36, 63-4
  specialisms 10
  support staff 10-11
accounts 48-51, 93-5, 101-2, 110-11, 114-7
  timed *see* annual accounts; monthly accounts
accrued expenses 72
accuracy 6, 22, 23
  petty cash 29
  see also errors
adjustment 71-4
administration, as expense 26
advertising, as expense 26
advice notes 54, 57
aged creditors' reports 101
aged sales ledger reports 101
annual accounts 7, 36-7, 63-77
application of funds reports 119-21
appropriation accounts 117, 118
asset stripping 77
assets 12
  fixed 25, 77
  and liabilities 104
  limited companies 74-6
  see also individual terms
auditors 10-11

B

Bad Debt Accounts 69, 72, 101
Balance Sheets 64-5, 75
balances, trial 63-4
bank accounts 6
  cheques 18, 20, 34
  separate for business 33-4
bank statements
  and books 34-7
books 5-6, 17
  and bank statements 34-7
  for cash transactions 18-20
  for petty cash 29
  for purchases purchase 22-7
  reconciliation 34-6
  for sales 20-2
  updating 20
budgeting 81-4
  from computerised systems 86-7
  safeguarding by 82-4

C

capital injection 12, 48-50
capital receipts 64
cash book 18-20
  and bank statements 18-20, 34-5

monthly financial reports 100-1

N

National Insurance 94-5

O

overdrafts 83

P

partnership accounts 117-8
Partnership Act 1890 116
partnership deeds 116-7
partnerships 111-2, 115
  limitations 116
  multiple functions 116
PAYE 95
payments
  late 55, 56, 58-9, 69, 72-3, 101
  prompt 71, 101
payroll 93-5
petty cash
  accuracy 28, 29
  cash boxes 27
  contra entries 29
  imprest method 28-9
  monthly accounts for 29
  vouchers 28, 29
premises
  asset stripping 77
  as expense 25

pricing
  and costing 84-6
  flexibility 85
  and stock 85
profit and loss 67-8, 77
Profit and Loss Accounts 69-71
profitability ratios 106-7
profits 58
purchase ledger reports 100-1
purchase ledgers 51, 56
purchase of business accounts 111
purchase orders 54
purchasing, of businesses
  failing concerns 109, 110
  going concerns 109-12

Q

quarterly accounts 7

R

ratio analysis 100, 101-8, 109, 110
reconciliation 34-6
remittance advice 54
rent accounts 72
repairs, as expense 25
retailers 19, 21, 37, 38-9, 41, 87

S

salaries 72, 93-5
sales ledgers 51, 56-9

More MADE EASY™ books...

Look out for the Professor! Made Easy Guides are practical, self-help business reference books which take you step by step through the subject in question.

- Legal and business titles
- Experts' advice
- 'How to' information and instructions
- Save professional fees!

Business Letters I & II

Business Letters I and *Business Letters II* are complementary Made Easy Guides, each providing an invaluable source of more than 100 ready-drafted letters for a range of business situations. Each letter has a useful commentary which helps you choose the right turn of phrase. The *Business Letters Made Easy* Guides take the headache and time-wasting out of letter writing, and provide you with letters that get results.

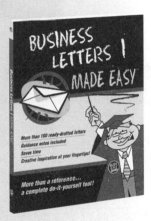

Code B504 • ISBN 1 902646 38 X • 250 x 199mm
paperback • 160pp • £9.99 • 1st Edition

Code B505 • ISBN 1 902646 39 8 • 250 x 199mm
paperback • 168pp • £9.99 • 1st Edition

Employment Law

Written by an employment law solicitor, *Employment Law Made Easy* is a comprehensive, reader-friendly source of information that will provide answers to practically all your employment law questions. Essential knowledge for employers and employees!

Code B502 • ISBN 1 902646 95 9 • 250 x 199mm
paperback • 168pp • £9.99 • 2nd Edition

... to order, simply call 020 7394 4040 or visit www.lawpack.co.uk

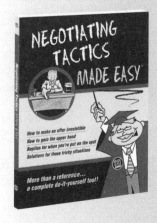